TALKING ABOUT AUTISM

1. Down the Rabbit Hole of Historical Controversies

Manuel F. Casanova M.D

Talking About Autism: *1. Down the Rabbit Hole of Historical Controversies*

Copyright © Manuel F. Casanova, 2023

First published in 2023 by Life & Learn.

All rights reserved. No part of this publication may be reproduced in any material form (including photocopying or storing in any medium by electronic means without the written permission of the copyright owner.

The views expressed in the published works do not express the views of the Publisher. The authors take legal and moral responsibility for the ideas expressed in the articles. The Publisher shall have no liability in the event of issuance of any claims for damages. The Publisher will not be held legally responsible should there be any claims for compensation.

A catalogue record for this book is available from the British Library.

ISBN: 978-1-7398181-2-8

www.lifeandlearn.net

I would like to dedicate this book to my oldest grandchild Bertrand "Buddy" Thomas Might. He was the first patient diagnosed with the rare disease N-glycanase (NGLY1) deficiency which provided for secondary autistic features. He left us with grace and dignity but always remembered as a boy who loved to smile and make others laugh; the world's best daddy to his pet fish; a lover of music, lights, and Elmo; someone skilled at snuggling and cheering others up; and the proudest older brother to his younger siblings. Buddy, my little bear, was a student at Mountain Brook elementary school where he excelled at making friends and touching hearts.

TABLE OF CONTENTS

PREFACE	1
INTRODUCTION	4
PART 1: AUTISM IN HISTORY	8
Autism and Childhood Schizophrenia	17
The Dark History of Autism	22
The Early Nazi History of Autism	29
The Nazi History Behind 'Asperger'	31
The Horrifying History of Hans Asperger	34
by Jill Escher	
The Invention of Autism in the Midst of Nazism	42
by Claudia Mazzucco	
George Frankl: The Unassuming Man Who Was Made Controversial	52
Frankl: A Third Man at the Genesis of the Autism Diagnosis	56
PART 2: BOOK REVIEWS	60
Neurotribe or Diatribe?	61
Reading Steve Silberman's book *NeuroTribes: The Legacy of Autism and the Future of Neurodiversity*	71
by Claudia Mazzucco	
In a Different Key: The Story of Autism	79

James Harris Discusses the Books *Neurotribes* and *In a Different Key*   84

PART 3: THE DARK SIDE OF PSYCHOANALYSIS   88

The Refrigerator Mothers	89
Therapy or Patient Abuse?	97
Fraud	102
The Direct Psychoanalytical Institute	108

PART 4: MISCELLANEOUS   115

Salt Lake City and its Role in the History of Autism	116
Memories of St. Elizabeths Hospital	121

CONCLUSION   129

About Author   133

PREFACE

Sometime in the early 1990s, a friend of mine, Charles T. Gordon III (nicknamed CT), approached me with the idea of establishing an organization that would promote research into autism. CT was the father of an autistic child and was distraught when considering that even though there had been major advancements in the neurosciences, not much was applicable or of benefit to his son's condition. CT placed me in contact with Eric London, who together with his wife Karen, were trying to fund the first organization aimed at accelerating biomedical research regarding autism. This was the beginning of the National Alliance for Autism Research (NAAR); friends helping friends in an organization wherein likeminded parents were dictating research initiatives. Nothing fancy about the early beginnings of the organization, with Eric coming to pick us up at the airport in his old station wagon and Karen doing most of the paperwork from the living room of their own home. Back then the overhead was practically nil, with most people participating in our brainstorming sessions with the good intention of seeing positive changes made in our nation's research infrastructure. Several years later when my first grandson was born, it became clear that he was on the spectrum. In the case of parents, the ubiquity of the condition explains why some people make reference to autism as a "pervasive" disorder.

Throughout the years I have been able to participate in many scientific advisory boards and autism support groups. My own basic research gradually shifted from Alzheimer's disease to schizophrenia and finally to autism. Along the way I was fortunate to meet many individuals that represented the very best of humanity. I have been humbled and honored in getting to know Steve Edelson, Jane Johnson, Terri Arranga, John Elder Robison, Jonathan Mitchell, Olga Bogdashina, Jill Escher, Katie Wright, Wenn Lawson, Stephen Shore and many others. These people are my heroes. We may not all share the same thoughts about autism, or the best ways to intervene, but we do keep their best interests at heart. I appreciate our differences and have tried to assimilate the positives from each of our different perspectives. It may be scary but challenging the *status quo* from our different viewpoints is essential towards moving forwards.

I am most grateful to my wife Emily Casanova. She thought that I needed a creative outlet for some of my academic interests. She assumed that this would ultimately focus on the history of medicine or electronics, but early on I decided to expand on my clinical interest in autism. Emily gave me a subscription as to WordPress as a Christmas present to start blogging (https://corticalchauvinism.com). I thought that writing on the topic of autism would convey to others not only some of my experiences, but also a passion for learning more about the subject. Raymond D. Adams, a towering figure in the field of

Neurology once said that diagnosis followed the three rules of real estate: location, location, and location. In my case, I have always thought that any pathological correlate of significance for autism would be most prominent within the cerebral cortex.

It has been said that gaining knowledge is the first step to wisdom, but sharing it is the first step to humanity. Autism is part of my life and I wanted to share my personal experiences with the reader. I think the small vignettes give an idea to my way of thinking. However, this is a "buyers be aware" scenario as anything that is so deeply personal is likely to be biased. In this regard, I have the baggage of my education as a physician, my contact with patients, and a lifetime of personal experiences that will always color my way of thinking. Given my travel and participation in different congresses and local meetings, I stand to further educate myself and mature in my positions from the experiences of others. In this regard, I welcome comments and especially personal stories, doubts and criticisms conferred to me during my lectures, webinars or in my blog.

Finally, I am most grateful to my four daughters. Each one of them has surpassed my expectations. Their character, goodwill, generosity, and spirit of self-growth have always inspired me. My first grandson Bertrand, nicknamed Little Bear, has reminded me that life itself is a miracle not to be taken for granted. Needless to say, the lives and struggles of our family fills me up with purpose and for that I am deeply grateful.

INTRODUCTION

Autism as a clinical entity has its origins from the clinical descriptions offered by both Leo Kanner and Hans Asperger sometime in the 1940s. Although both portrayed their patients as having deficits of social interaction, they disagreed on the nature of the condition. Kanner believed that patients in his clinical series suffered from a developmental condition; an innate malady giving rise to a lifelong disorder. To emphasize this point of view, Kanner would adjectivize the term as "early infantile autism". In contrast, Asperger ascribed the nature of the symptoms to a personality disorder. He called this an "autistic psychopathy" or a defect in the "thymic" of the personality. In Greek, 'thymos,' means the mind or heart as the seat of strong feelings or passions as well as being associated with internal psychological process of thought, emotion, and motivation. Both Kanner and Asperger described marked variability in clinical presentations and noted that, in some cases, characteristic behaviors of their patients were noticeable in their parents.

Autism as a diagnosis was not immediately accepted by the medical community. Many physicians believed that the varied symptoms observed in autistic individuals were the expression of childhood schizophrenia. According to the prevailing view of the time, autism was a childhood condition that manifested a progressively more chaotic interpretation of reality with aging. Difficulties with the diagnosis often happened because autism rarely occurred in pure form; rather, other psychiatric comorbid symptoms (e.g., mental retardation, hyperactivity, aggression) took diagnostic precedence in the minds of attending physicians. It is therefore unsurprising that some autistic individuals were subjected to a shotgun approach to therapy. Indeed, misguided attempts to alleviate schizophrenic symptoms in autistic children included electroconvulsive therapy (ECT) and lysergic acid diethylamide (LSD). At present, ECT is used for the relief of catatonic stupor in some autistic patients.

Controversies in autism have generalized outside medical practice to include social, political and economic issues. However, whenever there has been a controversy, there has been inquiry and subsequent growth. In all, the history of autism has been that of an evolving healthcare landscape. Especially in North America, age, sex, and insurance status as variables rarely provide appropriate intervention strategies. Modern medicine now requires a nuanced approach, personalized to the necessities of each autistic individual. If history teaches us anything is that a more personalized approach is also a more humane approach to healthcare.

This book is a collection of my (and others') posts on my blog https://corticalchauvinism.com/. The book is the first one in the series *'Talking About*

Autism' in what I hope will become a series of discussions about autism. The first conversation is that of the history and controversies surrounding autism. All statements express beliefs, but which of these can be proven true and which ones reflect a person's feelings? It will thus be interesting for the reader to consider what are opinions vs. facts, even when coming from professionals. As the reader of this book will learn, bridging the gap between facts and opinions in the history of autism is a controversial endeavor because both facts and opinions can be either successful or unsuccessful depending on the perspective of the individual.

The book is split into three parts:

Part 1 – Autism in History: Kanner, Asperger, Frankl

Part 2 – Book Reviews of *Neurotribes* and *In a Different Key*: what they did and didn't get right

Part 3 – The Dark Side of Psychoanalysis in relation to Autism

In each part, those that are 'guest' posts will be clearly stated and the authors have provided their consent for their work to be used in this book. References are provided at the end of each post.

What is said may not appeal to everyone but should certainly pique their curiosity. I hope that this book can provide the reader with an understanding for not taking things at face value and to think for themselves about certain topics.

Note: This book is written by an American author therefore the spelling is American-English and many references are U.S based.

PART 1: AUTISM IN HISTORY

We shall start, rightly enough, by looking at the 'diagnostic moment' which brought autism into the light of modern medicine. This was not the result of a pragmatic clinical trial but, rather, the epiphany of two professionals (Leo Kanner and Hans Asperger) who, although geographically distant from each other, shared a common cultural and educational heritage.

The term 'autism' was first introduced in 1908 by the Swiss psychiatrist Eugen Bleuler (1857-1939) to describe an atypical behavior observed in some schizophrenic patients. The etymology of the term "autism" stems from the Greek language: "autos", meaning self, and "ism", a suffix denoting a morbid action or state. Thus, the term denotes the behavior of 'being in oneself'; a description of a person who, for any given reason, withdraws from social activity. Bleuler observed clinical manifestations of autism in his schizophrenic patients when referring to the 'remoteness' that they kept. Indeed, many of his patients lived in a socially withdrawn and inaccessible manner prompted by what he considered to be an infantile wish to avoid reality. With time, other authors interpreted the initial concept in different ways and by the mid-1960s and onwards, they narrowed autistic withdrawal to a world devoid of symbolic life. These authors believed autism provided a life lacking in imagination; one incapable of understanding symbolic representations by way of humor and stories.

Michael Rutter, professor of child psychiatry and psychopathology (regarded as "the father of child psychiatry") in the United Kingdom, claimed that "the autistic child has a deficiency of fantasy rather than excess" (for a review, see Evans 2013). This misguided suggestion, attributing a deficient fantasy world to autistic individuals, was cast without considering the level of functioning or competence of diagnosed children nor the complex relationship that symbolic play has with multiple developmental domains.

Bleuler attempted to integrate the concept of autistic behavior along with symptoms indicative of inappropriate affect, ambivalence, and a loosening of thought associations in the diagnostic criteria for schizophrenia. His goal never materialized as autism is present only in a subset of schizophrenic individuals and is therefore not considered a central or core element of the condition.

Autism as applied to pervasive developmental disorders of childhood was probably first used by a medical professional in 1938 when Hans Asperger (1906-1980), a pediatrician at the Vienna University Hospital, used the terminology "autistic psychopaths" in a lecture, which he advertised as dealing with "The Mentally Abnormal Child". Six years later, Asperger published his habilitation, or doctoral thesis, entitled "Autistic Psychopathy in Childhood". The patients in this series were described as creatively intelligent but socially isolated. Other characteristics in the case histories included clumsiness, emotional poverty, special interests, stereotyped movements, and the use of elaborate and idiosyncratic language. Unfortunately, the contribution of Asperger remained largely unknown outside of the German literature until Lorna Wing replaced the expression autistic psychopath with its eponym (Asperger) in 1981. According to Schopler (1998, p.388), "Asperger's own publication did not inspire research, replication, or scientific interest prior to 1980. Instead, he laid the fertile groundwork for the diagnostic confusion that has grown since 1980". A decade later, Uta Frith translated Asperger's publication to English, and many suggested that some patients in the Asperger series echoed clinical features of a medical disorder contemporaneously reported by Leo Kanner.

Leo Kanner (1894-1981), born Chaskel Leib Kanner, is rightfully considered the father of autism. Born in Klekotow, Austria, Kanner pursued his medical education in Berlin with specialized training in cardiology. After emigrating to the United States in 1924, Kanner worked at the Yankton State Hospital in South Dakota (named Dakota Hospital for the Insane at its 1880 inauguration). At Yankton State Hospital, Kanner studied and reported on the effects of tertiary syphilis among Native Americans and the fluctuations in blood pressure accrued to changing levels of adrenalin (epinephrine) in patients with functional psychosis.

It may have been that the harsh arctic conditions in South Dakota swayed the Kanner family to seek refuge in other parts of the United States. Back then the most important item of a small home in the Dakotas was the stove, which was used for both cooking and heating. In the rural environment near major cities, small homes had a rope leading to the outhouse to prevent getting lost and ultimately dying during a heavy snowfall. It is, therefore, unsurprising that Kanner used his participation at medical congresses as a way of establishing professional contacts and garnering possible job offers. In an American Academy of Psychiatry Congress in Minneapolis, Kanner reached out to Adolf Meyer (1866-1950), the first psychiatrist-in-chief of the Johns Hopkins Hospital, asking for a job opportunity.

History turns on a dime. Four years after his arrival at the Yankton State Hospital, Kanner accepted a 3-year Commonwealth Fellowship at Johns Hopkins where he would reinvent himself as a psychiatrist. Under Adolf Meyer's influence, Kanner's diagnostic acumen would be refined by considering all possible biological, social and psychological factors of relevance to his patients. The copious notetaking required for this broad integrative diagnostic approach would be a strength in many of his future publications, a majority of which he wrote as sole or first author. After finishing his fellowship, Meyer enlisted Kanner's assistance in establishing the Children's Psychiatry Service at the Harriet Lane Home for Invalid Children. This happened as Dr.

Edwards A. Park became the Pediatrician-in-Chief of Harriet Lane. Under Park's long tenure, Pediatrics expanded into multiple subspecialties, many of which would bring deserved fame to Hopkins. In this way, Child Psychiatry flourished in the same environment that provided revolutionary advances, and established the world leaders in pediatric endocrinology, surgery and cardiology. The emphasis on psychobiology brought about by Adolf Meyer and Leo Kanner fell right in place with the scientific research and training being undertaken at Hopkins.

Sometime in 1942, Kanner was invited to be the guest editor for a special issue in a newly established journal named The Nervous Child. Having finished his training a few years before, the invitation may have been due, in part, to the professional networking capacity available to the Hopkins faculty. Ernest Harms, a clinical psychologist of European origin, served as the editor of The Nervous Child. The home base of the publication was Baltimore, Maryland, making the physical proximity to Kanner ideally suited towards establishing a friendly dialogue. Indeed, Kanner used Harms as a sounding board for his ideas. Kanner suggested to make this special issue around the theme of Affective Contact of Children. For his own endeavor, Kanner would collect a series of cases that had fascinated him for a number of years. One of the first cases had been seen in 1935 – a 3-and-a-half-year-old boy named David Speck, brought to Hopkins by his mother. By 1942, Kanner had collected a series of 8 children to which he added 3 more by the time of his publication.

It is noteworthy that the clinical series reported in Kanner's article has maintained its relevance through the decades and, according to Google scholar, has been cited 11,376 times (as of 10/25/18) within the medical literature. The journal of *The Nervous Child* in which this influential article was published, however, perished, closing production in 1956. Despite the international recognition Kanner received from his research and publications, he remained an Associate Professor at Johns Hopkins until his promotion to full Professor in 1957 at the ripe age of 63. Two years later, Kanner would retire and become an Emeritus Professor.

Kanner's seminal article published in 1943 described a series of children (8 boys and 3 girls, all under 11 years of age) initially diagnosed with childhood schizophrenia and/or emotional problems but who also exhibited an autistic withdrawal as originally conceived by Bleuler. These children existed in autistic isolation, living in a shell, keeping an anxious and obsessive desire for sameness, and exhibiting language and verbal rituals plagued by meaningless repetitions (echolalia). Many of the children described by Kanner had been diagnosed as "mentally weak", but curiously lacked any discernible cognitive impairment. Indeed, Kanner observed that his patients had an excellent use of vocabulary and an extraordinary memory for past events. Kanner concluded that the children were suffering from what he called "early childhood autism".

Although Bleuler introduced the term autism for schizophrenic patients, Kanner thought that these conditions were intrinsically different. Childhood schizophrenia was a psychotic disorder with a period of relative normalcy preceding the beginning of the illness and followed by a progressively deteriorating course. Kanner recognized clinical antecedent descriptions of the condition in the published works of Sukhareva (Russia), Lutz and Tramer (Switzerland), and Despert (United States). Thus, the symptoms were known, but whether these reflected the existence of a unique condition, deserving of an exclusive appellation, would have to wait for Kanner's analysis. Indeed, these antecedent reports failed to mention the term autism when describing the symptomatology. It may be that in Kanner's case, the conceptualization of the autistic behavior he observed in his patients came from long discussions with some of the parents of his patients. One of the mothers of his patients was a psychologist and another one a prominent pediatrician; moreover, four of the fathers were psychiatrists. Many of them lived close by, in the state of Maryland, enabling the possibility of frequent visits to the clinics (a review of the different patients in Kanner's series can be found in Olmsted and Blaxill, 2011).

It is noteworthy that one of the fathers was Wendell S. Muncie, a colleague of Kanner at the Phipps Psychiatric Clinics who also worked under the tutelage of Adolf Meyer. Wendell Muncie would go on to author the popular textbook, *Psychobiology and Psychiatry: A Textbook of Normal and Abnormal Human Behavior* (foreword by Adolf Meyer), which underwent 19 printings between 1939 and 1948. In his book, Muncie agrees with Kanner's reported observations, including the intelligence of the parents, alluding to the fact that one half of the families in the original series were represented in *'Who's Who in America'*, or in *'American Men of Science'*. Although autistic patients had been characterized as being unable to make intelligent decisions or judgements (feebleminded), Muncie believed that chronic acquaintance with them would disprove the claim. Autism was different and distinguishable from any other type of mental deficiency as well as childhood schizophrenia. According to Muncie, they looked intelligent and had, in some instances, phenomenal vocabulary and memory. Muncie's personal interest on the subject becomes clear when he cites observations from "unidentified parents" as to potential clinical findings for his medical textbook (e.g., the constancy of the autistic personality over the years). It may be that many parents, who were health-related professionals, provided copious histories, had been keen observers to signs and symptoms of significance, made reference to the relevant literature, and may have guided the discussions with Kanner as to possible diagnoses.

References:

Evans B. (2013) 'How autism became autism: the radical transformation of a central concept of child development in Britain.' *Hist Human Sci*, 26(3):3-31.

Kanner L. (1943) 'Autistic disturbances of affective contact.' *Nervous Child*. 2, 217-253.

Muncie W. (1948) *Psychobiology and Psychiatry: A textbook of normal and abnormal human behavior*. St. Louis: CV Mosby Company.

Olmsted D, Blaxill M. (2011) *The Age of Autism: Mercury, Medicine, and a Man-Made Epidemic*. New York: St. Martin's Griffin.

Schopler E. et al. (1998) *Asperger syndrome or high functioning autism? Current Issues in Autism*. 1st ed. Berlin: Plenum Press.

Autism and Childhood Schizophrenia

If you are having trouble getting answers for your symptoms, then you stand with most patients. Indeed it is commonly reported that only about 12 per cent of patients receive a correct diagnosis at their initial doctor's visit. The exact percentage for misdiagnosis is difficult to ascertain because usually there are no mechanisms for reporting them. Physicians usually establish a differential diagnosis based on medical history, laboratory tests and physical examination. When evidence does not clearly establish a diagnosis, a physician may adjectivize symptoms as abnormal or atypical. In some cases, diagnosis may be further camouflaged by symptoms that are partially absent or attenuated - the so-called *forme frustes*.

The early history of autism is marked by the uncertain characterization of the condition. Decades went by before key problems with its psychiatric diagnosis were overcome. A diagnostic system had to evolve that did not rely on personal biases but on operant definitions of behavior stemming from evidence-based practice. This is an evolving process that changes with our understanding of the underlying pathophysiology of a condition. In the case of autism, we still have a lot more to learn.

A few decades ago, after graduating from medical school, I learned that autism was considered to be a rare disorder. Back then, textbooks would report a prevalence of 1 in 10,000 individuals. Indeed, I remember one of my basic neurology textbooks stating that specialists would probably get to see one or two cases throughout the life of their clinical practice. I am not that old, I graduated from medical school in the late 1970s. Those medical textbooks were written some 30 years after Kanner had introduced the term to the literature. Still, a diagnosis of autism remained invisible to many clinicians. What was happening?

Contrary to my experience with autism by the time of my medical school graduation, I had already seen a couple of cases with a diagnosis of childhood schizophrenia. Such encounters were not considered uncommon. I remember reading some of the clinical accounts from Lauretta Bender in which she talked about her series: *'An experience of thousands of childhood schizophrenia cases'*. Bender was the psychiatrist who lent her name to the now famous Bender-Gestalt test. She trained at the Johns Hopkins Hospital before moving to New York and making her career at the Bellevue Hospital. During her lifetime, Bender was considered a force of nature. Other physicians would bow to her and defer to her opinion as dogma. This was rather unfortunate as many of her patients could easily have been considered autistics under modern diagnostic criteria. Even more unfortunate was the fact that Bender would use extreme measures in many of her patients as possible therapeutic interventions. This included the use of insulin shock therapy as a way of resetting the brain. Back then, Internal Review Boards (IRB) were not set in hospitals and patients were truly the guinea pigs of clinicians.

It really took somebody of courage to step up in the international arena and challenge the views of Bender. That brave soul was Leo Kanner. His debate with Bender was a respectful disagreement that transpired within the medical literature but never got personal. Both individuals knew each other from their training days at the Johns Hopkins Hospital and Bender even wrote one of the obituaries praising Kanner upon his death. In spite of their friendship, their disagreement ran for decades. The main objection for Kanner was that autism was a developmental condition; patients were born autistic! This trajectory differed markedly from schizophrenics that, according to Kanner, acquired and manifested symptoms sometime after birth. Curiously, this was the same reasoning that separated Kanner from Asperger in their case series. Asperger believed that symptoms were acquired after birth and represented a personality disorder.

Throughout the years the distinction between childhood schizophrenia and autism has remained fraught in controversy. Mice with a mutation of the Shank3 gene may serve as models for schizophrenia or autism depending on the type/location of mutation. Also, for some cases, catastrophic events may propitiate the expression of symptoms in both of these conditions. This is a well-known phenomenon in schizophrenia where many young individuals would exhibit full blown symptoms after leaving their social safeguards in order to go to college or army basic training. In autism, the same phenomenon has only recently received attention by clinicians. As part of the diagnostic criteria of DSM-5, we now stipulate that some autistic patients may develop their symptoms only after social exigencies overwhelm the patient.

In one of my series, from a state hospital in KY, a significant number of elderly patients who had been admitted as childhood schizophrenia patients had their diagnosis revised to autism. This series had some 10 patients, the youngest of which, at the time I examined them, was about 49 years of age. Unfortunately, institutionalization in these cases had grave consequences and many had lost a majority of their previous cognitive abilities. However, it clearly illustrated to me that autistic patients had always been albeit remaining invisible to medical diagnosis. In this regard, one of the many possible explanations to the rise on prevalence of autism is diagnostic substitution. Many patients previously diagnosed with childhood schizophrenia were actually autistic.

References

An article expanding on the shared symptoms and pathology between schizophrenia and autism: de Lacy N, King BH. (2013) 'Revisiting the relationship between autism and schizophrenia: toward an integrated neurobiology.' *Annu Rev Clin Psychol.* 9:555–587.

Bender L. (1947) Childhood schizophrenia; clinical study on one hundred schizophrenic children. *Am J Orthopsychiatry.* 1947 Jan;17(1):40-56.

Stone WS, Iguchi L. (2011) 'Do apparent overlaps between schizophrenia and autism spectrum disorders reflect superficial similarities or etiological commonalities?' *N am J Med Sci* 4(3):124-133.

The Dark History of Autism

In this and some of the following chapters I deal with the dark underbelly of autism. This was a dark history pitting good vs. evil: a political time that aligned clinical descriptions of autism with Nazi goals. In the Third Reich, physicians attempted to classify people as genetically fit or unfit and as to who should live or be killed. It is now apparent that Hans Asperger participated in some of these decisions. Fortunately, the DSM5 removed the Asperger eponym when designating some higher functioning autistic individuals.

It is striking that in today's society, the killing of minorities is sometimes condoned and that reverberations of euthanasia, as so-called "mercy killings", can be used to justify such measures. In the history of autism, Asperger rose to fame for having published a thesis describing the phenotype that bore his name. On the other hand, Asperger's role in the killing of dozens of handicapped children is less publicized.

Herwig Czech is an Austrian historian of war atrocities and a permanent research fellow at the Documentation Center of the Austrian Resistance. He also received an APART Fellowship from the Austrian Academy of Sciences.

The focus of academic interest for Mr. Czech has been the medical crimes committed at psychiatric hospitals during the occupation of the Nazi regime. His writings contest the official view of the role of Austria during World War II (Kandel, 2012). His work calls for remembrance of the many victims that, although dead, still have to receive justice. According to Czech, in a work published in English, Asperger kept a certain distance from the Nazi movement, which may account for the fact that his involvement in children's euthanasia remains practically unknown to this day. In 1942, as part of a seven-member commission, Asperger examined 220 inmates of the Gugging hospital's children's facility. Of these, 35 were sent to the Spiegelgrund at the behest of the commission; all 35 children died within a short period of time (Czech 2014). It is important to note that Am Spiegelgrund was a children's clinic implemented in 1940 after the Euthanasia Letter signed by Adolf Hitler. From 1940 to 1945, nearly 800 children perished at this institution, murdered by gassing or other methods. Am Spiegelgrund was headed by Erwin Jerkelius, a colleague of Asperger at the university clinic.

During World War II, euthanasia of handicapped individuals was more prevalent in Austria than in Germany. This may have been due to the fact that many of the patients in Austria were subjected to medical experimentation while they were alive or even after death (e.g., organ harvesting). Many of the physicians within such facilities used individuals as guinea pigs in lethal experiments (e.g., injecting them with virulent microscopic organisms like the one causing tuberculosis), while others investigated the use of medical technology to kill large numbers of individuals. Some inmates at these extermination facilities received a drug overdose, others were electrocuted, and those less fortunate were slowly starved to death. A significant portion of those murdered were children suffering from "idiocy" and/or diverse "deformities".

Let's be clear that inmates at these facilities were subjected to medical torture, including injections with apomorphine (providing hours of nausea and vomiting), painful injections of sulfur, physical isolation, and cold baths. After death, the children's brains and other organs were collected for further research. The body parts were then widely circulated among academic centers in Austria.

In one moment of historical hypocrisy, a perceived aim for research in the academic institutions of Austria was that of a movement trying to establish the field of therapeutic pedagogy as an independent discipline by joining different aspects of child psychiatry, psychology, and education. This emerging field had the laudable goal of providing occupational and play therapy, educational counseling, and accommodations as a means of "curative education". Each child was regarded as different, and the physician had to take into consideration social and predisposing factors as part of the treatment plan. Efforts to establish this new discipline united euthanasia activists from the Spiegelgrund, such as Erwin Jekelius and Heinrich Gross, with staff from the University Pediatric Clinic, such as Franz Hamburger and the now better-known Hans Asperger (Czech, 2014).

Several years ago, I had the pleasure of meeting the ever-gracious Eric Kandel who won a Nobel Prize for his work on memory. Kandel's family was forced to emigrate away from Austria leaving behind all their belongings. In his book *In Search of Memory* Kandel narrates that despite their active participation in the Holocaust, the Austrians claimed to be victims of Hitler's aggression - Otto von Hapsburg - the pretender to the Austrian throne managed to convince the Allies that Austria was the first free nation to fall victim to Hitler's war. Both the United States and the Soviet Union were willing to accept this argument in 1943, before the war ended, because von Hapsburg thought it would stimulate Austria's public resistance to the Nazis as the war ground to a halt. In later years both allies maintained the myth to ensure that Austria would remain neutral in the Cold War.

Because it was not held accountable for its actions between 1938 and 1945, Austria never underwent the soul-searching and cleansing that Germany did after the war. Austria readily accepted the mantle of injured innocence, and this attitude characterized many of Austria's actions after the war, including its treatment of Jewish financial claims. The country's initial uncompromising stand against paying reparations to the Jews was based on the premise that Austria had itself been a victim of aggression.

Equally disturbing was the fact that many of the non-Jewish members of the faculty of medicine who remained in Vienna during the war were Nazis, yet they retained their academic appointments afterwards. Furthermore, some who were initially forced to leave the faculty because they had committed crimes against humanity were later reinstated.

To give but one example, Richard Pernkopf, Dean of the Faculty of Medicine from 1938 to 1943 and rector of the University of Vienna from 1943 to 1945, was a Nazi even before Hitler entered Austria. Pernkopf had been a "supporting" member of the National Socialist party since 1932 and an official member since 1933. Three weeks after Austria joined Germany, he was appointed Dean; he appeared in Nazi uniform before the medical faculty, from which he had dismissed all Jewish physicians, and gave the "Heil Hitler" salute.

After the war, Pernkopf was imprisoned in Salzburg by Allied Forces but he was released a few years later, his status having been changed from that of war criminal to a lesser category. Perhaps most shockingly, he was allowed to finish his book *Atlas of Anatomy*, a work thought to be based on dissections of the bodies of people who had been killed in Austria concentration camps. (Kandel 2012)

Asperger was the most prominent physician connected to the history of autism and Nazi war crimes. However, there were other prominent physicians who were active parts of the Nazi machine and who have made contributions to the field of autism, as distasteful as it is. For example, Andreas Rett was an Austrian neurologist whose main claim to fame was the description of a syndrome that now bears his name. This syndrome affects primarily females and presents with a period of normal development (6 to 18 months of age), followed by loss or stagnation of developmental milestones, deceleration in brain growth, repetitive stereotyped movements, gastrointestinal disorders and seizures. Patients with Rett syndrome have intellectual impairment and typically lack verbal skills. It has been proposed that males may express a more severe condition and consequently die shortly after birth. Most patients with this condition exhibit a mutation in the gene MECP2. In the DSM-IV Rett syndrome was classified as a subtype of autism.

I participated in the first Rett Syndrome Center in the United States directed by Dr. Hugo Moser. Dr. Moser was a famous physician whose work was depicted in the movie "Lorenzo's Oil". Through Dr. Moser, I was able to interact with Dr. Rett who was always available to guide our efforts. Due to my training in both neurology and neuropathology, I shared a common academic interest with Dr. Rett. Overall, I found him to be very knowledgeable and otherwise, given his fame, to be unassuming. Back then, I was not aware of his participation or support of the Nazi regime.

I should add that, during the 1980s, while training at Johns Hopkins I was able to investigate neuropathological studies coming from Germany /Austria. Many of the researchers never cared about the origins of the samples used in their studies. I always thought that if the individual had died during the 1940s and they had a diagnosis of schizophrenia or were twins, the tissue could have probably come from concentration camps or euthanized patients in psychiatric hospitals. In many cases, the patients were tortured and neither they nor their relatives provided consent for tissue removal. Still their organs and tissues remained in jars without hope for proper burial. It took the German and Austrian governments nearly four decades after the war to raise consciousness and stop using this tissue - and then only after having been questioned on ethical grounds by scientists from other parts of the world.

References

Czech H. (2014) 'Abusive medical practices on "euthanasia" victims in Austria during and after World War II.' In S. Rubenfeld and S. Benedict (eds.) *Human Subjects Research after the Holocaust*, Springer International Publishing, Chapter 9, pp. 109-125.

Kandel E. (2006) *In Search of Memory*. NY: Norton and Company.

Kandel E. (2012) *The Age of Insight*. Random House

The Early Nazi History of Autism

According to Donvan and Zucker (2016), Asperger partook a role in the Nazi regime and was responsible for the death of an undetermined number of children. The person who discovered the connection and made it public was the Austrian historian of war atrocities Herwig Czech.

In 2014, Mr. Czech provided a lecture asserting the complicity of Asperger in the murder of dozens of children. Many people have claimed ever since that it is too early to take heed of Mr. Czech's findings, as the same has not been published and properly scrutinized. Some people, like Steve Silberman, have gone as far as to condone Asperger's actions despite, if proven, any possible involvement in murdering children during World War II. According to Mr. Silberman (2015), the most important lesson is not that brutal regimes like the Third Reich enable evil men to do evil, but that they are able to compel even well-intentioned people to do monstrous things. From my standpoint, there is no defense to the murder of innocent children whose only crime was suffering from some type of physical or mental disability.

Mr. Silberman's attitude and work ethics are in clear contradiction to those of Jon Donvan and Caren Zucker - the authors of *In a Different Key*. For the purpose of writing their book, Donvan and Zuker communicated regularly with Czech and then went to meet with him personally in Austria. During their stay in Austria, Czech accompanied them to the historical registries where the pertinent documents were archived. In part, the purpose of the trip was to examine the documentation detailing Asperger's involvement in war atrocities and to personally verify Asperger's signature in documents that condemned children to their death.

It does seem that Asperger's reported series of cases (1944) that now bear his name was very biased. The series (and his hospital population) reported a number of socially handicapped children who were all boys and exhibited gifts of various nature. The peculiarities of Asperger's clinical series can't be explained by statistical chance alone; rather, it appears possible that those children who were truly handicapped or whose only crime was being of the female gender may have been "euthanized" (murdered).

References

Asperger, H. (1944) 'Die "autistischen Psychopathen" im Kindesalter.' *Archiv für Psychiatrie und Nervenkrankheiten*, 117, 76-136.

1st Commemoration Lecture: Nazi Medical Crimes at the Psychiatric Hospital Gugging by Herwig Czech (the world lecture project (world-lecture-project.org), see lecture 47:09 time mark.

Donvan J., Zucker C. (2016) *In a Different Key: The Story of Autism*. NY: Crown Publishing Group.

Silberman S. (2015) *NeuroTribes*. AllenUnwin

The Nazi History Behind 'Asperger'

More claims are surfacing about the role of Hans Asperger with the Nazis and the execution of disabled children. Asperger was elevated to sainthood and proclaimed 'the Father of Neurodiversity' by Steve Silberman in *Neurotribes*. Silberman also defended the role of Asperger, once reports about war atrocities started to surface. In addition, the work of Mr. Silberman diminished the reputation of Leo Kanner who, in *Neurotribes,* is seen as a villain opposing Asperger. In reality, Kanner was a hero who saved hundreds of individuals during the war by helping them obtain asylum/citizenship in the United States.

The following paragraphs were taken from an opinion piece published in the New York Times by Edith Sheffer (Sunday Review, March 31, 2018). Ms. Sheffer is a senior fellow at the Institute of European Studies at the University of California, Berkeley, the author of Asperger's Children: The Origins of Autism in Nazi Vienna:

[The article is freely available to read/download for those interested-
https://www.nytimes.com/2018/03/31/opinion/sunday/nazi-history-asperger.html]

"As Asperger sought promotion to Associate Professor, his writings about the diagnosis grew harsher. He stressed the "cruelty" and "sadistic traits" of the children he studied, itemizing their "autistic acts of malice". He also called autistic psychopaths "intelligent automata". Some laud Asperger's language about the "special abilities" of children on the "most favorable" end of his autistic "range," speculating that he applied his diagnosis to protect them from Nazi eugenics — a kind of psychiatric Schindler's list."

Note by Manuel Casanova: While people were resigned to the normalcy of the Holocaust (i.e., the genocide of European Jews) during the Nazi regime, Oskar Schindler decided that fate was a matter of individual choice and focused on saving as many Jews as he could].

"But this was in keeping with the selective benevolence of Nazi psychiatry; Asperger also warned that "less favorable cases" would "roam the streets" as adults, "grotesque and dilapidated.""

Asperger worked closely with the top figures in Vienna's euthanasia program, including Erwin Jekelius, the director of Am Spiegelgrund, who was engaged to Hitler's sister. My archival research, along with that of other scholars of euthanasia like Herwig Czech, the author of a forthcoming paper on this subject in the journal *Molecular Autism*, show that Asperger recommended the transfer of children to Spiegelgrund. Dozens of them were killed there.

Another opinion piece was provided by Andrew Griffin, which, in no uncertain terms, states that,

> "Documents uncovered by an Austrian medical historian suggest that Prof. Asperger ingratiated himself with the Nazi regime to the extent of participating in its murderous euthanasia programme." It claims that Asperger sent profoundly disabled children who were under his care to the Spiegelgrund clinic, where they were killed. An estimated 789 children, many with severe mental problems, were systematically killed at the Vienna clinic, mostly by lethal injection and gassing. Others died from disease and starvation, or were subjected to harsh medical experiments."

References

Griffin A. (April 2018) 'Pioneering autism doctor Hans Asperger sent disabled children to be killed by Nazis, new study claims' *Independent* –
(https://www.independent.co.uk/news/science/asperger-nazi-study-latest-proof-hans-autism-research-spiegelgrund-a8311181.html)

The Horrifying History of Hans Asperger

by Jill Escher

The following piece is written by Jill Escher (an autism research philanthropist, president of Autism Society San Francisco Bay Area, autism housing provider, and mother of two children with nonverbal forms of autism).

A new book by Bay Area scholar of German history, Edith Sheffer tells a detailed, grisly story of the Nazi disability death machine and the role within it played by Hans Asperger, the Vienna clinician for whom the now defunct diagnosis of "Asperger's Syndrome" was named.

Asperger's Children: The Origins of Autism in Nazi Germany is a chilling masterpiece of modern history, embroidered with layers of detail and insights that make it an invaluable resource for anyone wishing to understand how the Nazi creed of racial hygiene resulted in the unspeakable horror of the sterilization, torture, and murder of countless thousands of children and adults with physical and mental disabilities.

For those interested in the history of autism, however, its relevance is questionable. Indeed, the book is almost an argument for why Asperger's actual work, as opposed to the post-hoc mythologizing of it, has so little bearing on today's understanding of autism. The "autism" of Asperger is actually his term "autistic psychopathy," an amorphous and variable politico-psychiatric concept referring mainly to impulsive and nonconforming behavior. From Asperger's rough description of this ill-defined trait, combined with his own admissions of irrelevance, the origins of "autism" as we know it today in 2018 can hardly be said to have a root in wartime Vienna.

In the psychiatry of the time, the word psychopathy pointed to malice, trouble-making, delinquency, and rebelliousness; it was a word imbued with the potential for criminality. And "autistic" was an adjective to describe a lack of social connectedness. Asperger never delineated much in the way of criteria for his autistic psychopathy — based on Sheffer's account, it was at best a nebulous concept grounded in failings of "Gemüt," a term used to describe a fascistic social spirit and the capacity for conforming to social norms.

Asperger's descriptions of his autistic psychopaths (only four are described in his 1944 paper, one of whom had brain damage) brought to mind not our modern concepts of autism so much as what we today might label: Oppositional Defiant Disorder, Attention Deficit Hyperactivity Disorder, or Conduct Disorder.

Sometimes brain damage, genetic or metabolic disorders, or even Fetal Alcohol Spectrum Disorder seemed to be at play with these children. It's too easy to get derailed by the "autism" in "autistic psychopathy," and presume relevance to today's "autism" when the intention was rather different: Asperger was concerned with a personality disorder, not a developmental disorder.

Sheffer also relates how Asperger's concept of autistic psychopathy was politically motivated, thinly researched, poorly documented, shifted over time, and was basically a footnote in his overall career. His vague notions would not have made much of a dent in the annals of psychiatry were it not for British psychiatrist Lorna Wing's 1981 article suggesting Asperger's population as a variant of Kanner's autism. This was over Asperger's own protests — he saw a distinction between the extraordinarily capable boys (Asperger saw his psychopathy as exclusively male) he described and the developmentally disabled children of Kanner's population. Even Wing later felt she had erred. "I would like to throw all labels away today," Sheffer tells us she said before her death, and said she preferred a move towards a dimensional approach.

But surely Asperger's work must have some relevance to the history of autism, no? I certainly have a hard time finding it and, in truth, after reading this excellent and devastating book, it hardly seems important. The glory of Sheffer's book lies not in any attempt to fulfill the promise of its subtitle, but rather in its exceptionally rich treatment of the ghastly horrors arising from the eugenics-driven Nazi mandate to purge outliers and "sick genetic material" from the Volk. For example, Chapter 8 offers a detailed account of life at Vienna's infamous Spiegelgrund where children suffered starvation, torture, freezing conditions, sadistic discipline, horrific experiments, and open views of handcarts filled with children's corpses. Children, who by today's standards had no or very little disability, were murdered: foster children, poor children, children of single mothers, children who wet the bed or couldn't complete test puzzles, or had delinquency. The unworthy would often die by murder instigated by barbiturate poisoning, the brutal consequence of which was thinly disguised as death by "pneumonia." The concept of "autistic psychopathy" is but a tiny footnote to the overall parade of horrors.

What seems to be most important to Sheffer, however, is this: the Third Reich's collapse of humanity would not have been possible without guiding principles and authorities defining how to apply them. It often fell to the psychiatrists of the Third Reich to determine which young people of post-Anschluss Austria qualified as members of the new Volk, and which, due to their disabilities or non-conforming behaviors, should be eliminated through sterilization or murder, sometimes referred to Spiegelgrund or other nightmarish facilities. Asperger's autistic psychopathy was one of many conceptual tools for helping to rate and rank Austrian youth. At the close of the book, the author prompts readers to consider the effects that labels can have on people's concept of self, and on society's concept of them.

Unlike medical practice of today, which is grounded in the Hippocratic Oath; physicians under the Nazis aimed to promote the collective strength of the supposedly biologically superior Aryan nation rather than the health of any given individual. During the Nazi era, when Asperger, or his brethren at the University of Vienna Children's Hospital and elsewhere, evaluated a child, it was largely in the service of the eugenic dream and not in order to promote the welfare of the patient. Those with "inferior hereditary material" were viewed as a "burden on the community" and were to "be eliminated." As noted by Asperger's mentor and hospital director, Franz Hamburger, "Excessive care of the inferior allows inferior genetic material to circulate." By implying superiority or inferiority, labels in the Reich had life-or-death consequences.

Asperger described autistic psychopaths as either worthy of remediation and inclusion in the Volk, or more seriously disabled and therefore unworthy. The former were described as highly intelligent, with "astonishingly mature special interests," and "originality of thought" capable of "outstanding achievements." For those valuable autistic psychopaths, he sought to restore them "their place in the organism of the social community," drawing on Nazi phraseology. However, "in the majority of cases," he wrote, "the positive aspects of autistic traits do not outweigh the negative ones." The less desirable ones could be "nonsensical, eccentric, and useless." Those unfortunates had an "inability to learn" and an "unfavorable social prognosis." He likened the more intellectually impaired to automatons, and worse, "waste." It does appear that the vast majority of the people considered to have the disorder of autism today would have been relegated by Asperger and his colleagues to the pseudo-medical death squads.

So why were some boys saved? Even the satanic Erwin Jekelius, the "overlord with the syringe," as the Royal Air Force called him, and director of Spiegelgrund, lauded Asperger for his effort to rehabilitate those "who have been marginalized." Why? As Sheffer noted and historian Herwig Czech (2018) emphasized in his paper), the Reich needed men to fill jobs, and potentially useful young males to be assigned to productive roles was part of Asperger's and the hospital's mission. Though some historical revisionists have painted Asperger as a hero for saving some young lives, both Sheffer and Czech make it clear Asperger's participation in the murderous regime was in the service of Nazi goals, and an active choice on his part.

While most of the book is in the nature of a dense academic treatise, at the close, Sheffer switches gears to engage in a rambling search for a moral, a lesson that could be relevant for today's disabled, or for her own son, who, we are told in the Acknowledgements, has been diagnosed with autism. For me, these lessons sprang to mind:

The name: The name 'Asperger' had fairly neutral connotations for me until reading Zucker and Donvan's *In a Different Key*, and now Sheffer's and Czech's work. The name now fills me with nausea, evoking a strange, complicit man who willingly, and perhaps eagerly, worked as a cog in the Nazi crusade to purify the Volk, sending innocent children to their deaths. I have little doubt it should be dispensed from the official vocabulary of mental disability and difference (and indeed it has). Whether individuals wish to continue to use "Aspie," "Aspergian" or other terms in informal parlance should, however, be entirely up to them. I would even argue that "Aspie" to mean a socially challenged, science-geeky kind of kid or adult has taken on a life of its own, quite divorced from the Nazi-era psychiatrist's work and legacy.

Labels: As mentioned above, Sheffer, who is a historian of Germany and Central Europe, a Senior Fellow at the Institute of European Studies at the UC Berkeley, is concerned about the impact of applying labels to children with developmental and cognitive challenges. Personally, I like clinical labels only to the extent they actually result in real, tangible help to patients. Labels that confer little or no meaningful benefit to suffering individuals deserve exit. I don't find the term "autism" very useful to that end and would agree with Lorna Wing that a dimensional approach would be better. Too much is made of the word "autism" or "autistic," somewhat blinding us from seeing the complex genomic, neurodevelopmental, and functional realities of individuals who need our help. Incidentally, there is already a bit of movement toward the dimensional approach, which can be detected in the ICD-11's new autism rubric structured by intellectual and communication ability.

Niemals Vergessen: Watching the rise of a nouveaux fascism here in our own country, one cannot help but shudder at the idea that the principles of Nazi psychiatry could rise again. Thankfully, Sheffer's extraordinary work solidly echoes the clarion call engraved on a memorial at Spiegelgrund, exhorting us to "Niemals Vergessen," or "Never Forget."

[This review was originally published at sfautismsociety.org/blog July 9, 2018.] Disclaimer: The opinions and assertions stated herein are those of the individual author and may not reflect the opinions or beliefs of Autism Society San Francisco Bay Area or the Autism Society of America.

References

Czech, H. (2018) 'Hans Asperger, National Socialism, and "race hygiene" in Nazi-era Vienna.' *Molecular Autism* 9:1–43. (https://molecularautism.biomedcentral.com/articles/10.1186/s13229-018-0208-6)

Shefferis E. (2020) *Asperger's Children: The Origins of Autism in Nazi Vienna.* W. W. Norton & Company.

The Invention of Autism in the Midst of Nazism

by Claudia Mazzucco

The following piece is written by Claudia Mazzuco. Ms. Claudia Mazzucco is a writer, researcher, historian, editor and teacher of the history of golf. She was born in Santiago del Estero, Argentina, and was diagnosed with autism in the summer of 2001 in London. Claudia is an advocate of the notion that it is worth knowing the differences between the symptoms of possible autism and problem behaviors that look like autism but are not. At the root of a spectrum that keeps getting bigger and bigger, she concluded, is the tendency in American society to categorize an increasing array for normal childhood reactions to stressful life situations as proof positive of a neurological disorder. She supports very strongly scientific research, both for curing autism and helping individuals with Asperger Syndrome to find acceptance and integration.

In 1942, the world was a hellish place when Austrian pediatrician Dr. Hans Asperger submitted to Vienna University his postdoctoral thesis (published two years later). Adolf Hitler had outlined – in 1924 – a political philosophy for a new Aryan state based on a combination of blood, soil and National Socialism. The party platform was filled with passion, pomposity, paranoia, and anthropological ideas that purported to uphold the superiority of the Aryan race over others, in particular the Jewish race. Nazi propaganda filtered into Austria and anti-Semitism was gaining a foothold throughout the country. It was a time of racism to an insane degree, laws of sterilization, eugenics and euthanasia policies, and seriously misguided notions of intelligence and human heredity. The truth of the matter, Edith Sheffer (2020) said, was that:

> "The Third Reich was a diagnosis regime, obsessed with sorting the population into categories, cataloging people by race, religion, politics, sexuality, criminality and purported biological, mental and behavioral defects. Nazi officials created massive population indexes that compiled individuals' medical, financial, educational, criminal and welfare records — even sports club files. By 1942, Reich Health Leader Leonardo Conti estimated that ten million Reich citizens had been indexed — 12% of the total population. These files, then, established the grounds for sterilization, deportation and extermination."

Hitler did spark a world war with fifty million dead, massacred six millions Jews, set up the Gestapo, and so forth. No subject within the Reich was free from politicization. Neurobiology and psychology had been under ideological attack for years. The National Socialist party established its pedagogic goals and demanded that it be the only valid one.

In 1938 – on the eve of World War II – Dr. Asperger wrote an article 'The Mentally Abnormal Child' that presents two boys. The first boy was "intelligent far beyond his age" but suffered from mental and physical "over-sensitivities" – no link to autism. The second represented the first case of an "autistic psychopath" in medical literature, as Herwig Czech reports in 'Hans Asperger, National Socialism, and "Race Hygiene" in Nazi-Era Vienna'. He suffered from a "profound disorder of the personality," although he exhibited – like the first boy – "a contrast between pathological and in some ways valuable traits."

Dr. Asperger had spent pivotal years of his career in Nazi Vienna. He managed to become a member of the Bund Neuland, a Catholic youth organization focused on outdoor activities, with roots in the German Youth Movement. He was someone the party could count on, and that is how it turned out at the Vienna University Children's Clinic. But he was not a Nazi; he was a man who performed his duty honestly and without shirking. The world needs to reorganize itself both intellectually and spiritually, he said. Not least in medicine. This simple sentence is sufficiently vague to contain the universal anxiety about such reorganization, mixed with the universal hope that it would actually happen. It is not National Socialism he embraced, but its anti-individualistic and totalitarian approach to medicine and health.

Change has seized all areas of this life. "The central idea of the New Reich," Asperger said, "that the whole is more than its parts, and that the Volk is more important than the individual, had to bring about fundamental changes in our whole attitude, since this regards the nation's most precious asset, its health." And yet, he sees the problem not from the standpoint of the Volk as a totality but from the standpoint of the abnormal children.

It is true that Dr. Asperger recommended permanent placement at Spiegelgrund of Herta Schereiber, a little girl – two months shy of her 3rd birthday – who he examined at his clinic on June 27, 1941, but she died of pneumonia two months and six days later (on Sept 2). (Dying from pneumonia was the common diagnosis for those who had been overdosed with barbiturates.) We rebel at this conclusion but also demur on grounds that, in the direst of circumstances, there was a paucity of medical supplies, no antibiotics, and no treatment that could help her survive. Herta showed signs of "severe motoric retardation and personality disorder, an excessive degree of idiocy and seizures." A few months before, she had fallen ill with encephalitis. Spiegelgrund was a psychiatric hospital in Vienna, which during the war became a collecting point for children who did not conform to the regime's criteria of hereditary worthiness and racial purity. Her mother asked to be notified if the condition of her child should get worse. She could see for herself that the child was mentally not well. If she could not be helped, it would be better if she died. She would not have anything in this world, she would only be ridiculed by others.

There was an acute fear of ridicule in a society permeated by contempt for the unworthy life and the social stigma of mental disability. Similar stories were found in the Soviet Union even after the death of Stalin in 1953. "One arrested physician," William Taubman (2017) said, "the well-known pathologist Yakov Rappoport, later recalled the mother of a child with pneumonia, who refused to administer the penicillin prescribed by a doctor: "Let him die from illness, but not from poison that I gave him with my own hands."

As a pediatrician, Dr. Asperger was an advocate for his children's interests. However, his prognoses for the "autistic psychopaths" were far from universally optimistic. He did not highlight their potential but rather contrasted them unfavorably with other, less impaired patients. He emphasized that the condition varied greatly in terms of "social prognosis" and "worthiness." While he deemed some of the "autistic psychopaths" capable of "great intellectual achievements," in other cases, "autistic originality" was deemed "bizarre, eccentric, and useless," with "fluid transitions towards schizophrenia" whose "main characteristic is also autism, the loss of any contact with the surroundings." He treated troubled children with the utmost dedication to help them overcome their challenges. He advocated on their behalf, defending their value as human beings, and calling for loving care for each of them.

But there is a limit. Dr. Asperger was intensely absorbed on the questions 'concerning the inheritance of mental traits and mental abnormalities,' leading the way "in the practical tasks of eugenics, especially with regards to the problems relating to the Law for the Prevention of Hereditarily Diseased Offspring." He studied the influence of optimal environmental conditions on 'hereditarily burdened individuals,' as he put it. He sought to attribute mental troubles to constitution rather than environmental factors. Genetic makeup determined primarily an individual's possibilities of mental development. However, he did appreciate the importance of education "in spite of inheritance," concluding that it is worth the trouble with individuals outside the norm. The most important question for him was: How much can we accomplish for these children?

On a Spectrum that is more about strong emotion than solid evidence, is it not time for researchers to put a fresh set of eyes on the very definition of autism to be sure that we are talking about the same thing? For example, it was not a "small miracle," as Uta Frith (1991) said, that a young doctor was captivated by these difficult children; there was an urgency to Dr. Asperger's work that left little room for scientific curiosity or idle – purely speculative – theories of autism. It was a matter of state and of the utmost importance: the worthiness of human beings. He felt so strongly for his patients with autism that he explored every possible path of recovery.

> "We think that such individuals have their own place in the organism of the social community, which they fully occupy, some of them maybe in ways nobody else could. […] Such individuals show more than others what capacities for development and adaptation even abnormal personalities dispose of. Often, in the course of development, possibilities for social integration arise which one would not have expected before. […] This fact determines our attitude and our value judgment towards difficult individuals of this and other kinds and gives us the right and the obligation to stand up for them with the whole force of our personality."

As Dr. Asperger thought it, I would have to admit that his clinical insights about autism are surely akin to those of my own pediatrician, Dr. Nazario. What matters most about Dr. Asperger is not that he discovered autism before Kanner did, but that he speculated that there is inherent resiliency in the constitution of the brain. He was indeed dropping the barriers of determinism. "To our own amazement, we have seen that autistic individuals," Dr. Asperger said, "as long as they are intellectually intact, can almost always achieve professional success, usually in highly specialized academic professions, often in very high positions, with a preference for abstract content " (Asperger in Frith 1991).

A simple and righteous man, Dr. Nazario was also enough of an armchair psychologist to understand that not being the most sociable child in the neighborhood was not a big deal. Dr. Asperger had established as the essential feature of the condition that autism was a disturbance of adaptation to the social environment. "They are strangely impenetrable and difficult to fathom," Dr. Asperger said, "Their emotional life remains a closed book."

Dr. Nazario could not refute it openly because my grandma confirmed that I was oblivious to my surroundings. It began to seem plausible to him that I might have autism but "psychopathy" (or clinical idiocy) was also the applicable word to denote autism as a disparity from normal functioning. For my pediatrician, that was absurd and destructive. Not knowing what the condition really was, he said to my grandma, "You think this, you think that, but let's try to educate these children. Whatever is wrong with them might be fixable." She then started believing that autism would be manageable. I was seven years old already, and very receptive to education.

Although Dr. Asperger felt empathy for abnormal children, he understood autism as a childhood psychopathy; specifically, he designated a group of children with distinct psychological characteristics as "autistic psychopaths." The modern description of Asperger's Syndrome is essentially social clumsiness. The one has nothing to do with the other. How can one reconcile Kanner's description of autism as an innate inability to form the usual, biologically provided contact with people with Asperger's syndrome that recognized autistic traits in verbally fluent individuals who demonstrate superior intelligence and creativity? It is also hard to understand how such verbally fluent individuals could demonstrate superior intelligence and creativity without establishing some sort of contact with the world and its people. To accomplish verbal fluency does require us using language to record the ongoing discovery of the world, and thus develop our intellect and originality.

Lorna Wing got it all wrong. The problem is not chiefly the fact she tried to keep Dr. Asperger utterly separated from the Nazi Regime but that she had obviously not studied his postdoctoral thesis deeply enough. As a result, the bridge between her insights and research and those of Dr. Asperger is weak. According to Simon Baron-Cohen and Francesca Happe, "her epidemiological work at the Medical Research Council Social Psychiatry Unit at the Institute of Psychiatry in London demonstrated the clustering of social and communication impairments with lack of pretend play (replaced by repetitive behavior and interests) that marked autism as a syndrome." Dr. Asperger's narrative makes no reference whatsoever to lack of pretend play, and the neurocognitive deficit in theory of mind.

Sometimes the best way to reject those who contradict us is by converting the other to our views. Did Wing realize that she made a lousy adaptation of Dr. Asperger's paper? How could Wing support creating an Autism Spectrum Disorder that would include individuals who obviously did not show the traits of "autistic psychopathy" described by Asperger's account? No wonder, modern diagnosis in ASD has resulted in 'There is something wrong with this kid. Look in the DSM to find out what it is. Don't trace the signs to any real experience from the outside.' Ultimately, what the diagnosis could take away from him is the truth about himself. For when an 8-year-old does not present developmental issues, the reason that makes him "troublesome" or mentally imbalanced is not to be found in his genes or in a brain built wrong, which certainly is the main characteristic of Kanner's autism.

References

Asperger H. (1938) 'Das psychisch abnorme Kind.' *Wien Klin Wochenschr*. 49:1314–1317.

Frith U (ed): (1991) *Autism and Asperger Syndrome*, p. 7; ch 2: 'Autistic Psychopathy in Childhood', p. 87, Cambridge, UK: Cambridge University Press.

Sheffer E. (2020) *Asperger's Children: The Origins of Autism in Nazi Vienna*. W. W. Norton & Company.

Taubman W. (2017) *Gorbachev: His Life and Times*. New York & London: W.W. Norton & Company, p. 45.

George Frankl: The Unassuming Man Who Was Made Controversial

In his book, *Neurotribes*, Steve Silberman discovered that George Frankl went to work with Kanner after previously having worked with Asperger. From there on, it is suggested that Kanner had stolen the diagnosis of autism from Asperger by having Frankl act as an intermediary. According to Simon Baron-Cohen (2015), "Frankl had crossed the Atlantic and Silberman's argument is that Kanner heard about these special children in Vienna, found similar ones in his Baltimore clinic, and repackaged them as his own discovery."

Kanner acknowledged in his publications that Frankl worked with him at Hopkins. What is open to discussion is whether Frankl was able to mentor somebody of Kanner's stature. Hopkins faculty members were talented clinicians with diverse training in a world-class academic institution with a rich European tradition. It seems quite likely that anybody at the Hopkins Department would have given Frankl a run for his money.

The Hopkins Psychiatry Department was established by Adolf Meyer and from early on developed a tradition of intermixing both European ideas of psychoanalysis with the biological foundations of neurology and neuropathology. This was the Department where Lauretta Bender did some of her initial research before going to establish herself in New York as the world's leading authority in childhood schizophrenia. She directed the Children's Psychiatry services at Bellevue Hospital for 21 years starting in 1934. Lauretta, a figure of great influence in psychiatry, wrote one of Kanner's academic obituaries. The obituary concluded with the following words, "Leo Kanner maintained a lifelong enthusiasm for helping troubled children and their parents. His patients enjoyed, as did his professional colleagues, his uniquely piquant scholarly concern and the empathic relationship he always established" (Bender 1982). In their writings, it is evident that Bender and Kanner had a mutual admiration society. It was at Hopkins that Lauretta met Paul Schilder, MD, PhD, her future husband. Paul, an Austrian psychiatrist who immigrated to the Unites States, worked along with Lauretta diagnosing and treating psychotic children and publishing a large number of articles before his untimely death from a traffic accident at fifty-four years of age.

At Hopkins, Frankl was an interesting addition who could have received mentorship from others but probably not the other way around. His few years at the institution were rather undistinguished and his writings in regard to the emotional disconnect observed in some children denote some major confusion as to pathophysiological mechanisms.

Although highly praised by Kanner, Frankl lacked the biological tradition forged at Hopkins and eventually moved on after a few years to head a small Child Psychiatry clinic in Kansas City.

Kanner believed that the condition in his case histories and those described by Asperger were different. Kanner described classic autism as being present at birth thus classifying the same as a neurodevelopmental disorder – in this belief he was unwavering. Asperger thought his own cases represented a personality disorder developed or forged during the lifetime of the individual. He explained the use of the word psychopath as a personality disorder in the introduction of his article. Unfortunately, this part of the article was never translated to the English language.

While Kanner was taking steps to report his patients, Frankl was at a loss on how to describe the condition and whether it was in any way different from childhood schizophrenia. Contrary to Kanner and Asperger, Frankl never took a stance as to whether autism was a neurodevelopmental condition or a personality disorder. His interest, if anything, focused on non-idiopathic cases which differed remarkably from Kanner's classical autism. Frankl never mentored Kanner because he had reached no major conclusions of his own and had no ideas to teach. His citation index was poor and his work was never acknowledged as being of potential significance. Indeed, it was Kanner who first brought up the subject of autism in a letter to the mother of his incept patient and later on developed a differential diagnosis as well as recognizing antecedents within the medical literature (Donvan and Zucker 2017). As Kanner worked on his cases and prepared his publications, Frankl had already passed away many years into oblivion.

It would be wrong to take any major conclusions from Asperger's work and generalize them. Any astute clinician would find it very odd that after seeing a significant number of patients, the case histories in Asperger's reported series were all males, higher functioning, and having significant gifts and/or abilities. This is a biased series for anybody who has taken care of institutionalized patients. It now appears more evident that the bias in his series probably reflected the fact that the Third Reich eliminated those potential inmates who were primarily females, lower functioning and lacking in gifts or useful abilities. Thus, although Asperger recognized the gifts in some autistic individuals, those lacking the same may have been euthanized. It is unfortunate that Asperger's cherry-picked series has now been taken over as a way of conceptualizing some attributes of autistic individuals.

References

Baron-Cohen S. (2015) 'Leo Kanner, Hans Asperger, and the discovery of autism.' *The Lancet*, 386(10001):1329-1330.

Bender L. (1982) 'In memoriam Leo Kanner.' *Journal of the American Academy of Child Psychiatry*, 21(1):88-9.

Donvan J., Zucker C. (2017) *In a Different Key: The Story of Autism*. Broadway Books.

Frankl: A Third Man at the Genesis of the Autism Diagnosis

John Elder Robison's article 'Kanner, Asperger, and Frankl: A Third Man at the Genesis of the Autism Diagnosis' was published by the English publishing house Sage in their journal *Autism*. It is a lengthy 10-page original article that bears on the historical coincidence of two Austrians, Kanner and Asperger, coming to describe different tail ends of the severity of the autism spectrum while using the same terminology borrowed from Bleuler. In this regard, Robison points to the possible influence of Georg Frankl acting as a middleman between Kanner and Asperger.

I was very impressed with the quality of John's article. It marks a transition for John Elder Robison, the bestselling author of different autobiographical accounts turned into a serious investigative journalist. The main point of the article is that Georg Frankl went from working with Asperger to working with Kanner and was brought to public attention by Steve Silberman in his book Neurotribes. However, John Robison expands on the story and gives a detailed documentation of this transition based on work he did at the Johns Hopkins archives, genealogical databases, Ellis Island immigration documents, and a large number of articles in the medical literature.

At least in terms of Kanner, the queries about how he came about diagnosing autism, bear in part on how he recruited his original series of patients. I must say that even though a lot of credit has been given to Silberman, Donvan and Zucker for bringing to light the medical record of Donald Triplett (patient 1 for Kanner) from Johns Hopkins, very little praise has been bestowed on the person who originally discovered and published the same. This was the work of Dan Olmsted who published a series of articles on the subject in 2005. His main discovery was how Donald was given gold salts to treat a crippling disabling juvenile arthritis. The treatment was not recorded by Kanner, but according to Donald's brother, the treatment cured his arthritis and some of the affective symptoms associated with his autism. In 2011, Olmsted and Blaxill published in a book the story of Donald along with all other participants from Kanner's original series. This was several years before Silberman, Donvan or Zucker published their efforts.

What I like about Robison's story is the ideas by which he ties Frankl's love affair with Ami Weiss and brings it to play in the diagnostic controversy involving Kanner and Asperger. In doing so, Robison talks about the Nazi prosecution of the 1930s, Kanner's generous nature as a sponsor of many refugees, Frankl's contributions to the medical literature, and how the dreams and jobs of all of these important people became entangled at a particular chronological singularity.

Personally, I like many of the insights offered by John Robison. One of them was the possibility that Asperger saw higher functioning individuals because, at the time, the Third Reich would have involved lower functioning ones in their euthanasia movement and killed them. Robison is also careful to point out the importance of many Jewish physicians in the early history of autism, as well as in clearly defining some of the controversy involving the use of translated terms and their etymology. Lastly, I would like to point out that many of the clinical observations provided by John Robison are as astute as they are relevant. John is a very insightful individual.

Personally, I disagree with the importance given to Frankl in the history of autism. However, I must praise John's effort in giving a balanced appraisal on the subject. The story he pieced together reflects several years of investigative efforts. This is a must read for anybody interested in the history of autism. They will find that 10 pages are too short and that you are left wanting more. I wish this was the beginning of a book with a historical account from John's own viewpoint.

References

Olmsted D (2005) 'The age of Autism: The Story so far' https://www.upi.com/Health_News/2005/12/17/The-Age-of-Autism-The-story-so-far/39891134853162/

Olmsted D, Blaxill M. (2011) *The Age of Autism: Mercury, Medicine, and a Man-Made Epidemic.* New York: St. Martin's Griffin.

Robison JE. (2017) 'Kanner, Asperger, and Frankl: A third man at the genesis of the autism diagnosis.' *Autism* 21(7):862-871

PART 2: BOOK REVIEWS

In the next section we will take a look at two different books, *Neurotribes* and *In a Different Key*. Both offer an extensive account of the history of autism from very different perspectives while effectively communicating their message and providing voluminous source materials to validate their claims. Silberman's account is relentless as he chases the history of autism into biased corners and mantra repetitions. In this regard, the author uses historical biographical accounts as examples of autistic individuals and their achievements in society while simultaneously hammering the need for societal accommodations. The account is meant to be inspirational but, after several hundred repetitive pages, it becomes overdone. By way of contrast, Donvan and Zucker's account is a mix of factual and anecdotal stories parceling information at the right clip. It is clear that both Donvan and Zucker act as investigative reporters wilding a straightforward narrative loaded with exposition. Both books provide for rather extensive reading but each chapter crackles with enough excitement to captivate the reader.

Neurotribe or Diatribe?

I finally got a chance to finish reading Steve Silberman's widely publicized book *Neurotribes*. The book received the prestigious 2015 Samuel Johnson prize for non-fiction and some journalists have touted it as the definitive book on autism's past. Being a history buff myself, I decided to give it a try and read it.

The book itself has been proclaimed to be Neurodiversity's manifesto and as such, makes de rigueur claims of historical figures as having had Asperger's, providing a putdown of psychiatry and medical sciences in general, and somehow managing to talk peripherally about homosexuality and/or transgender issues. The aim of such a divagation is to ascertain that autism spectrum disorders are an expression of normal variability within the human genome and that any handicaps attributed to the condition can be overcome with proper accommodations. If this were the case, it is easy to see why Neurodiversity proponents downplay the need for treatment and research and find especially offensive the use of Applied Behavioral Analysis (ABA). In order to sustain their allegations, they claim that autism has always been around and that there has been no real increase in prevalence throughout the last few decades. They also tend to over-generalize suggesting that a significant proportion of engineers, radio aficionados, science fiction buffs, and computer scientists fall within the autism spectrum. All of the aforementioned allegations are made without dwelling on arguments that can falsify their position while simultaneously trying to destroy the credibility and reputation of those who oppose them. In their exposition they will usually not provide references to their work, or in the case of Mr. Silberman, those given may be untraceable and therefore worthless. *Neurotribes* touches on all of the aforementioned aspects while following the Neurodiversity blueprint to a tee.

The book glorifies autism by exalting its gifts but failing to emphasize its handicaps, drawbacks or comorbidities. It is true that the author mentions that autism is a handicap but at the same time equiparates the disability to computers using different operating systems, one with Microsoft and another using Linux. This comparison trivializes many of the handicaps faced by autistic individuals and is offensive to those more severely affected.

In the following paragraphs I will summarize Kanner's way of thinking by using his own words. I am providing the quotes from Kanner's articles in their entirety, as the original publications may not be available to most readers.

> "By this time, it should be – but very likely is not – quite commonplace to state that one of the combined goals of medicine, psychology, social work, and education is to make it possible for

children to attain their optimal condition of comfort and smoothness of functioning. No matter how simple this formulation sounds, civilization took a long time to arrive at it, and to many people and in many areas, it still has the ring of novelty. We are, after all, not too far behind from the era of the rod and the dunce cap and the bending of the twig to insure the haphazardly preordained inclination of trees". (1)

"Particular emphasis should be placed on the adjective "optimal" contained in the formulation. The optimum which can be reached is, of course, not identical to each individual…[he] can be helped if we examine the specifics of the underlying disharmony of the integrants and work for a better consonance between them." (1)

"The concept of operant conditioning occasionally has been misapplied; in precious zeal, this approach to therapy has been championed as a foregone success on the basis of what are in fact, fragmentary attainments." (2)

Kanner opposed characterizing individuals based on psychometric tests, again emphasizing the individuality of the subject:

"These terms, if taken literally, seemed to imply that the scores, meant originally to assess a child's anticipated adaptation to classroom instruction, represents a measurement of his "psyche" or "mind". Needless to say that this is glaring fallacy. There is more to psyche or mind that a few items of cognition selected for a clearly circumscribed purpose." (1)

Kanner's defense of children was both personal and emotional; furthermore, his quest for accommodations far anteceded that of the Neurodiversity movement. In this regard he advocated for parents to accept their children for whom they were, not whom they wished they could be:

"I recall a number of children who, being told how well they had done in a series of tests, implored me prayerfully not to report this to their parents. They had been told much too often at home and at school that they owed it to their endowment to do better and that their failure to equate achievement with tested potential must be ascribed to laziness, stubbornness, self-imposed lack of motivation, or what have you. To the child's own quandary about himself is added opprobrium of the all-knowing adult's disapproval." (1)

"Billy could indeed do better, not if- as the phrase has it- "he only would", but if his circumstances had made it possible for him to do better, if there were no depressants of his native ability arising from any number of equally significant integrants." (1)

"Slowly, gropingly, we are in the process of learning how to evolve practical ways to increase the comfort and productivity of those whose progress has been lessened by shortcomings of the physical and social integrants of maturation." (1)

Kanner promoted the civil rights of the individuals to be themselves (a right to their identity regardless of medical appellations). In a certain sense Kanner can be considered the father of the civil rights movement for disabled individuals which is now attributed to the Neurodiversity movement:

"This is the place to retell the story of Willy. Willy was the scion of a noted scientist father and a college graduate mother. He was in good physical health; socio-economic conditions were satisfactory; his I.Q. was phenomenally high. He absorbed erudition like a sponge. Already in pre-adolescence he achieved national fame as a wondrous child prodigy. At 12 years, he delivered a much-admired lecture before a distinguished audience of university notables. No one seemed to notice that Willy had no companions, that he was bewildered, lonely, and miserable in a world in which the everyday pleasures of childhood were denied. Oversaturated, Willy threw all his learning to the winds, rented a room in a large metropolis, and spent the rest of his life as an obscure office clerk. When he died at 48 years of age, all that he left behind was an album of transportation tokens, the collection and mounting of which had become his interest." (1)

"In the last few millennia our species has had its gifted and productive thinkers and poets and artists and scientists and explorers. Many of them have advanced our civilization by upsetting deep-seated archaic notions guarded zealously and at times cruelly by mighty autocracies of one kind or another. We are now in a position to spot potential talents at an early age and have the laudable desire to see to it that as many as possible reach their optimum. We can do this only if, as they mature, we as parents, educators, and human engineers can pave their way toward the developments of unhampered automaticity. It is up to us, then, to attenuate the hampering agents, be they organic, emotional, or social, and to encourage rather than crush, spontaneity and self-organization." (1)

"I wish I could say that the Willys, the Stevens, and the Jacks are exceedingly rare exceptions. But they are not. They are some of the casualties of the neglect of their right to their right of identity, being given no opportunity to think and to plan for themselves, painfully reacting to the kind of upbringing which does not differ too much from computerization and carrying with them the unmitigated results of the disharmony of the integrants of personality." (1)

Kanner's explanation as to the term refrigerator parents:

"From the start I was greatly impressed with one observation which stood out prominently: The parents of these patients were, for the most part, strongly preoccupied with abstractions of a scientific, literary, or artistic nature, and limited in genuine interest in people. As time went on and more autistic children were studied, the coincidence of infantile autism and the parent's mechanized forms of living was really startling. This was confirmed by many other observers. I noted then, however: These children's aloneness from the beginning of life makes it difficult to attribute the whole picture exclusively to the type of early parental relationship that they have experienced....At no time have I pointed to the parents as the primary, postnatal sources of pathogenicity." (2)

Kanner was prompt to criticize the parental blame game stemming from his original description:

"The children's aloneness from the beginning of life makes it difficult to attribute the whole picture exclusively to the type of the early parental relations with our patients." Later on, he would go on to say: "Approximately 10% of the parents did not fit the stereotype, besides, those who did reared other normal or, at any rate, nonpsychotic offspring. Moreover, similarly frigid parents are often seen whose children are not autistic." (3)

It should be stressed that Kanner was the psychiatrist who stood up pre-eminently (1968) to criticize Bettelheim at the height of the latter's popularity and prestige. In the following text Kanner mocks any conclusions attained by Bettelheim:

Kanner regularly dealt with the differential diagnosis of autism, specifically as applied to schizophrenia (3). For his efforts he received the Stanley R. Dean Research Award to the outstanding scientist for major contributions to basic research on schizophrenia. He claimed childhood schizophrenia was a rare condition and that many of the patients so diagnosed in reality fell into an assortment of neuropathological identifiable, more or less progressive, congenital or acquired anomalies of the central nervous system. He differentiated childhood schizophrenia from infantile autism as the former was a psychotic disorder with a deteriorating course. Kanner recognized clinical antecedents of autism (3, 6) in the works of Sukhareva (which he also noted being spelled Ssucharewa) in Russia, Lutz and Tramer in Switzerland, and Despert in the USA but despite similarities he distinguished the aforementioned as being different conditions:

> "It was deemed essential for the diagnosis in both groups that a period of relative normalcy had preceded the beginning of the illness." (3)

Having some knowledge on the subject, I thought that *Neurotribes* was a painful read. Silberman's arguments are constructed as a house of straws. It is very naïve to accept accounts of Asperger's achievements and political views coming from biased parties (i.e., his daughter). The well-publicized story that Nazis came to arrest him twice and he was only saved by the intervention of his supervisor was his own assertion. I have to wonder how many people in the postwar era tried to distance themselves from the Nazis with a similar story.

We all believe in accommodations. Some of us fight for them while others only talk about them. Personally, I believe that research efforts by the federal government and private funding organizations have been misguided. Research should be prioritized as to those efforts that can create a difference in patient's lives now rather than later. Still, I support research and attempts at improving treatment options. Opinions like those in *Neurotribes* may only serve to provide a negative impact on these efforts.

References

(1) Kanner L. (1971) 'The integrative aspects of ability.' *Acta Paedopsychiatrica,* 38(5):134-44.

(2) Kanner L. (1968) 'Infantile autism revisited.' *Psychiatry Digest,* 29(2):17-28.

(3) Kanner L. (1965) 'Infantile autism and the schizophrenias.' *Behavioral Science,* 10(4):412-420.

(4) Kanner L. (1965) 'Children in state hospitals.' *American Journal of Psychiatry,* 121:925-927.

(5) Kanner L. (1973) 'The birth of early infantile autism.' *Journal of Autism and Childhood Schizophrenia*, 3(2):93-95.

(6) Kanner L (1971) 'Childhood psychosis: a historical overview.' *Journal of Autism and Childhood Schizophrenia,* 1(1):14-19.

(7) Kanner L. (1971) 'Editorial: Retrospect and Prospect.' Journal of Autism and Childhood Schizophrenia, 1(4):453-459, 1971.

(8) Kanner L., Rodriguez A., Ashenden B. (1972) 'How far can autistic children go in matters of social adaptation?' *Journal of Autism and Childhood Schizophrenia,* 2(1):9-33.

(9) Olmsted D., Blaxill M. (2016) 'Leo Kanner's mention of 1938 in his report on autism refers to his first patient.' *Journal of Autism and Developmental Disorders*, 46(1):340-341.

(10) King M, Bearman P. (2009) 'Diagnostic change and the increased prevalence of autism.' *International Journal of Epidemiology*, 38(5):1224-1234

(11) Irva Hertz-Picciotto. (January 3, 2012) 'Commentary on the LA Times series on autism'. http://blog.autismspeaks.org/tag/irva-hertz-picciotto/

See also: Kanner L. (1941) *In Defense of Mothers*. 2nd edition. Mead Dood publisher.

Reading Steve Silberman's book *NeuroTribes: The Legacy of Autism and the Future of Neurodiversity*

by Claudia Mazzucco

What does Dr. Hans Asperger say about autism? The answer is: it is not schizophrenia. Autism is not some isolated deviation from acceptable behavior that was found floating out there in the ether. The roots of autism are partially embedded in the highly imaginative speculation of modern psychology. It is too obvious that Dr. Asperger had become acquainted with the term "autism", which appeared in German language writings before eventually moving into English and other languages. The Swiss psychiatrist Eugen Bleuler (1857–1939) was the first to use this term in a 1908 speech. Later, Bleuler said in 'Dementia Praecox' (1911) that "autistic schizophrenics" are "the most severe schizophrenics, who live in a world of their own." Here the formal entrance of autism as a characteristic of schizophrenia is of uppermost concern, for it provides the proper context within which to discuss the work of Dr. Hans Asperger.

Let Asperger Be A Pediatrician

We must let Dr. Asperger say what Dr. Asperger meant. First, we can only discuss what the paper of Asperger actually contains, not what we would like it to. He sought a fundamental difference and proposed to use the label autism for, and only for drawing a distinction between the abnormal personality structure of the children he was concerned with and the fundamental disturbance of contact that is manifest in an extreme form in schizophrenic patients. "Autism is the paramount feature in both cases," he wrote. "Essential symptoms of schizophrenia and the symptoms of our children can thus be brought under a common denominator: the shutting-off of relations between self and the outside world. However, unlike schizophrenic patients, our children do not show a disintegration of personality. They are therefore not psychotic." (Asperger in Frith 1991, p.39)

Autism in the Time of Nazism

Second, to let Dr. Asperger say what Dr. Asperger meant, I've argued earlier that Dr. Asperger's fundamental commitment to this "type" of children must be situated within the Austrian transition from perpetrators to victims, and that his conviction that autistic people have their place in society, must be seen not only as a response to the terrors of the Gestapo but, more importantly, as an effort to make good on his duties to set a boundary between normality and mental disorder. Here I would like to suggest that we should read Allen Frances's mea culpa book *Saving Normal: An Insider's Revolt Against Out-of-Control Psychiatric Diagnosis,* in a similar light. The coming of Nazism was catastrophic for Austria. During the Nazi occupation (from March 12, 1938 to 1945), children were exposed to a terrifying experience that they could not handle. Children react to war in a variety of ways. Emotional detachment and aggressiveness, indifference and disobedience, seem well justified by the circumstances. What could have gone wrong in Asperger's children was the whole process of personal adjustment to the war and its circumstances. They found themselves isolated, betrayed, bewildered, and maybe even depressed. Their deviations from acceptable behavior could also have been due to acute post-traumatic stress disorder.

Dr. Asperger was fundamentally committed to his children in the time of National Socialism in Austria. We must not forget that many of his colleagues were part of the most extreme killing project, the most extreme human degradation in a regime of brutal racism. These children often differentiated themselves from others in the way they were capable of "dereistic thinking." Bleuler intensified speculation concerning the nature of autistic or dereistic thinking by explaining it as guided by desires and affects and not goal directed. "Apart from schizophrenia, which it is at its most bizarre," Dr. Asperger wrote, "autistic or dereistic thinking can also be found in people who are not psychotic, and indeed in everyday life, for example, in superstitions or pseudo-science."

To reiterate: Dr. Asperger did not discover autism first. He explained autism only in relation to schizophrenia. Thus, he was not victimized by Leo Kanner who buried him in history – really, when you think about it, a highly improbable and infamous story – Kanner did not obscure the breadth and diversity of the spectrum because it is unlikely that Asperger experienced autism as something different from childhood psychopathy. It will always remain of cardinal significance to me that they both agreed in the essential conviction that autism was not an early form of schizophrenia. Again, Asperger's work shows that there were no clinical signs of "progressive deterioration" and he did not expect irreparable psychotic breakdown in these children. "In essence, they remain the same throughout their life," Asperger said, "though there is often improved adaptation, and many can achieve a reasonable degree of social integration." Steve Silberman's book, *NeuroTribes*, while important, impressive and admirable in many ways, took creative license on these and other issues.

Third, before reading *NeuroTribes*, readers owe it to themselves to read 'Autistic psychopathy in childhood', by Hans Asperger, translated and annotated by Uta Frith (1991). Silberman affirmed that Dr. Asperger "saw autistic people as a subset of humanity that had accelerated the evolution of science and technology." That description is nowhere to be found in his paper, because in the first place, Asperger did not put forward ideas about an "umbrella diagnosis" that covered profoundly disabled children and others who, in spite of their difficulties, come across as very bright.

Among the grounds for misreading his paper, one particularly prominent example, was that his children were not disabled. His first case was a boy called Fritz V.

Fritz had an excellent apprehension of a situation and an accurate judgment of people. "He quickly learned to express himself in sentences and soon talked like an adult." But "he shows a very severe impairment in social integration." He felt puzzled and uncertain, as I also did, because he noticed the characteristic manifestations of autism were "not at all rare in children, especially in their milder form." In short, Asperger's autism (or this type of abnormally developing child) could be mitigated not through psychological treatment but by understanding, love and guidance. There was no reason for Dr. Asperger why these children could not achieve professional success, "as long as they are intellectually intact."

Neither did Dr. Asperger expand the concept of autism to be a lifelong condition lasting "from birth to death," as Silberman affirmed, not to be just a childhood disorder. That "they were a hidden thread in the weave of culture, and had always been here," is unequivocally Silberman's own train of thought, unrelated to the original work of Hans Asperger. It is highly probable that when Dr. Asperger spoke of the "persistence over time" of the autistic personality type, that was only to indicate that the condition of the child was not degenerating into schizophrenia. For, if profound social problems do not overshadow everything else, but are compensated by a high level of original thought and experience, one thing must follow: their relation with society could be dealt with in an intelligent way, but only when they could fulfil their social role within the community, especially if they find understanding, love and guidance. The self and the world need not be in conflict.

Did Dr. Asperger call these children "little professors"? Certainly, he did not. It is important to add that in Dr. Asperger's account there is nothing, not a single reference to "little professors." When Fred Volkmar, a child psychiatrist at the Yale Child Study Center, was conducting a large research project on Asperger's syndrome in the 1990s, he distinguished children with Asperger [syndrome] from autism by their linguistic precocity. "Unlike the linguistically impaired autistics of the type depicted in the movie "Rain Man", Asperger's children talk like little professors. They seem brilliant because they have this language," Volkmar said to British writer and novelist Laurence Osborne. "But in reality, it's fact-obsessed, fact-oriented. It's rigid and insular. It's not a social brilliance. Usually, their social interactions are a disaster." In his book of 2002, *American Normal*, Osborne called children with Asperger's Syndrome "little professors," a description all the more instructive in its introduction, no doubt sympathetic of Asperger's sufferers.

Conclusion

Not that I look down on Silberman for having pursued the neurodivergent as an ideal. I am quite entertained by his efforts to make regular people look different. Most of what commonly passes for autism (or high-functioning autism) nowadays is clinically not autism at all. In my view, the concern with being different is the result of a double illusion. But my amusement arises from the unavoidable disparity I see between what a "neurodivergent" person is imagined to be and its real character. He has taken artistic license with facts, shaping them so a coherent story will unfold with a beginning, middle, and end. What is most resonant here – and Silberman is representative – is the great distance between modern America and Dr. Hans Asperger. He said, "The more that I discovered about Asperger's conception of autism, the more it struck me as incredibly prescient." That is hardly the case. It does not ring true to those who have already read Dr. Asperger's paper. I completely agree that Asperger feared that his patients were in danger of being sent to Nazi extermination camps. Yet all too often the recollection of the past is plainly created on the spot.

The very act of writing about Dr. Hans Asperger and his time is seventy years removed from the events he is recreating. This, however, did not prevent Silberman from assuming he really did know, that he really can describe them in full detail – just because the book contains such a gigantic bibliographical index – and this is how *Neurotribes* began. That is all a great, beautiful confabulation without which the story could not go on.

References:

Asperger H. (1991) 'Autistic Psychopathy in Childhood' in Frith U (ed) *Autism and Asperger Syndrome*, Cambridge, UK: Cambridge University Press.

In a Different Key: The Story of Autism

At first, I had misgivings about reading the book by Donvan and Zucker, *In a Different Key*, detailing aspects of the history of autism. Nowadays efforts by journalists often offer a biased perspective aimed at selling books rather than anything else. Furthermore, when considering the size of the book (over 600 pages), I thought the story would unravel in tangents that ultimately contribute little in terms of the subject at hand. My preconceptions originated from having read the book *Neurotribes* by Silberman, a journalist who massaged historical facts in order to publicize Neurodiversity's credos.

My preconceptions about Donvan and Zucker's new book were ill-founded. This is a must read for anybody interested in autism. The book is a well-balanced exposition giving the positives and negatives of many aspects of autism; for example, the authors praise Asperger's work as a clinician but simultaneously expand on his role as a murderous criminal within the Nazi regimen. They also give appropriate credit to AutismSpeaks but then detail some (not all) of the controversies that have followed. Other juicy details, for example, IMFAR's first meeting, occurred behind closed doors and may not have been accessible to the authors.

The book *In a Different Key* is not the complete history of autism; such an endeavor would have required several thousand pages. However, I liked the fact that the authors didn't only go after the lowest-hanging fruits but engaged themselves in a good amount of investigative reporting for which the book is carefully annotated with references. Instead of attaching labels to historical figures and partaking in flights of the imagination, Donovan and Zucker investigated autism's historical antecedents in the blessed fools of Russia, Hugo Blair (a case report by Uta Frith), feral children, etc. As an aside, I thought that feral children (those raised in the wild) as illustrated by Victor of Aveyron, although having a claim in the history of autism (see Frith 2003), should have been carefully delineated. In the end, feral children are not autistic.

The book reinforced my profound respect for the founders of the National Alliance for Autism Research (NAAR) and Cure Autism Now (CAN). I belonged to the first advisory board of NAAR in 1994. I remember Eric London coming to pick me up at the airport in his old station wagon. NAAR was for many years a mom-and-pop operation with an overhead of only a 5%. This would drastically change when they joined AutismSpeaks. Simultaneous with Eric's efforts, Portia Iverson from CAN was making a presence for autism everywhere. I was surprised when one day she called me after publishing an article on minicolumns and autism in order to learn more about the discovery. Among her many achievements, not the least, was the fact that she brought Tito Mukhopaadhyay and his mother Soma to the United States. Soma herself introduced the Rapid Prompting Method to our country thus helping hundreds of individuals within the spectrum.

Despite all of the positives, I thought the book offered an anglophile's perspective on autism by limiting its descriptions to events that happened within the United States and England. Christopher Gillberg is mentioned in passing but many international luminaries, for example Maria Isabel Bayonas, are missing. England may have had the first National Autistic Society but Spain closely followed. APNA had its first international autism congress in 1978 with 1,800 delegates attending from all over the world. Among the plenary speakers at the congress were Bernard Rimland and Ivar Lovaas. Similarly, a chapter detailing the success of communities of autistic individuals should have been included. At present, Mas Casadevall has been operating in the small village of Serinya, Spain for some 27 years. Similar efforts have followed in England and more recently in the United States.

Furthermore, I believe that Donvan and Zucker's book should have devoted more attention to the DSM controversy. The story of a scientific article from Yale that raised concerns about the exclusion of many people with an autism diagnosis could have been better explained. The scientific article per se jumped the gun in re-analyzing data based on criteria that had not yet even been approved or published by the DSM-5 committee. The authors would have probably gained some insight as to the personal tug of war that happened by interviewing Sue Swedo, the person who headed the DSM-5 committee. For those interested in reading more, see Gary Greenberg's *The Book of Woe*.

Although, not necessary to discuss, one of my personal peeves in the history autism involves cases of regression. Once considered very rare, it is now acknowledged that they entail a significant portion of cases. This recognition, as well as many other facets of autism, (e.g., sensory problems) that are presently only being re-discovered in the medical literature have been, in part, due to the combined efforts of parents and autistic individuals.

I loved reading this book. It was at times funny and at other times gut wrenching. I truly empathized with some of the stories in the book. My own grandson, Bertrand or Little Bear, was expelled from an expensive private school because the teachers did not believe that he could be taught. At present, he is toothless not because his teeth were extracted due to self-injurious behaviors but because of bruxism. Bertrand, my little bear, still wears diapers, needs help when feeding, and suffers from multifocal seizures. Two of my daughters moved closer to Little Bear's mother to help raise him. When it comes to a severely impaired child it sometimes takes a tribe to help raise them.

I am happy that some authors, contrary to Mr. Silberman, take the plight of my grandson and those of similarly affected families seriously. *In a Different Key* is a thoughtful exposition of autism. Knowing a good amount on the subject, I did not notice major flaws, only positives. To the authors I express my gratitude for putting the history of autism in perspective and humanizing the efforts of both parents and autistic individuals.

References

Frith, U. (2003) *Autism: Explaining the Enigma*, 2nd edition, Wiley-Blackwell.

Gary Greenberg (2014) *The Book of Woe: The DSM and the Unmaking of Psychiatry*, Plume.

For those interested, another good book on the history of autism is that of Adam Feinsten (2010) *A History of Autism: Conversations with the Pioneers*. Wiley-Blackwell, 2010.

James Harris Discusses the Books *Neurotribes* and *In a Different Key*

Jim Harris (2016) wrote a critical review of two published books dealing with the history of autism. One of the books reviewed was *Neurotribes* written by Steve Silberman and the other was *In a Different Key* written by John Donvan and Caren Zucker. The book review was published in the Journal of the American Academy of Child and Adolescent Psychiatry (JAACAP) and the issue was introduced by an editorial written by Andres Martin entitled: 'Leo Kanner and Hans Asperger: Setting the Historical Record Straight.' As a side note, Dr. Mark Gilbert, who is Kanner's grandson, for purpose of the book review, gave permission to JAACAP to reproduce a portrait of Kanner that is privately owned by the family.

It is of interest to note that Jim Harris is the Director of Developmental Neuropsychiatry for the Johns Hopkins Hospital and the Kennedy Krieger Institute. He is the author of my favorite textbook in neurosciences, a 2-volume treatise on *Developmental Neuropsychiatry* that won the Medical Book of the Year Award for 1996. Dr. Harris has won numerous awards for his continuous work on intellectual disabilities but, most importantly, Dr. Harris knew

Kanner personally and what his patients and their families thought about him.

I must say that I sensed a certain amount of what could be called justified anger on part of Drs. Martin and Harris from their written pieces. The same was directed at Steve Silberman, the writer who chastised Kanner and elevated Asperger to Sainthood as the proclaimed founder of Neurodiversity. The main conclusion from Dr. Harris' review being that Mr. Silberman fudged the interpretation of historical facts/accounts in order to benefit his own biased account of Neurodiversity and how this biased perspective stood in counter position to the more balanced historical account offered by John Donvan and Caren Zucker.

The book review starts by elucidating the role of Leo Kanner in the history of Child Psychiatry. It emphasizes his advocacy for social justice and ethical treatment for those with intellectual disabilities, his belief that treatment should be individualized to the needs of each individual, and his stance against euthanasia – the latter in clear contrast to Asperger who actively participated in the euthanasia movement. In *Neurotribes*, Silberman attacks Kanner's character rather than impartially discussing the available historical facts. Through Silberman's eyes, Kanner is seen as acting in "typically grandiose fashion", and that his "capitulation to his powerful peers was as swift as it was brutal to parents." According to Harris, Silberman writes that Kanner was a scientist who, by blaming the parents, "made the syndrome a source of shame and stigma worldwide while sending autism research off in the wrong direction for decades." He then spends a distressingly long time suggesting that Kanner plagiarized Asperger through Dr. Frankl (a mutual acquaintance that worked in tandem for both of them). According to Dr. Harris, Silberman is wrong in all of these accounts.

Kanner always believed that autism was born of an innate proclivity, a view embraced by present day science and multiple neuropathological and genetic studies. This view is too difficult to swallow for Silberman who upon upholding Neurodiversity's credo tries to portray autism as a result of normal variability within the human phenotype. To uphold Kanner's view, Mr. Silberman would have to agree that autism is a medical condition with grave implications for many individuals. Moreover, the fact that Frankl may have helped Kanner formulate his diagnosis of autism in a way that mimicked that of Asperger lacks credence. Frankl was primarily preoccupied with non-idiopathic types of autism, not the classical autism formulated by Kanner. Furthermore, even Asperger recognized that Kanner's autism was different from what he had formulated.

Dr. Harris offers more severe criticisms of Mr Silberman's portrayal of Asperger with data primarily derived from John Donvan and Caren Zucker in interviews with the Austrian historian of war atrocities Mr. Herwig Czech. According to Dr. Harris,

"Donvan and Zucker present a more balanced view of Kanner's and Asperger's contributions but, unlike Silberman, make clear Asperger's compliance with the National Socialist Party (Nazis) in Vienna. They challenge Silberman's portrayal of Asperger as resisting the Nazi agenda. There is evidence (Herwig Czech, personal communication, February 28, 2016) that Asperger took an oath to Hitler and accepted his racist policies. Silberman does acknowledge that to keep his hospital position, Asperger would have been required to sign a loyalty oath to Hitler. Each time Asperger applied for a post or a promotion, he was cleared as someone who, although not a party member, abided by Nazi principles in the performance of his job. In one instance, a party official wrote that he "conforms to the principles of the policy of racial hygiene" (Herwig Czech, personal communication, February 28, 2016).

Czech presented this information about Asperger's complicity with the Nazis at an Asperger retrospective in Vienna in 2010 and published his findings in 2011 and 2014." Dr. Harris book review is full of references that can be checked, including those of Herwig Czech.

References

Harris JC (2016) 'NeuroTribes: The Legacy of Autism; In a Different Key: The Story of Autism' *JAACAP*, 55[8]:729-733.

Martin A. (2016) 'Leo Kanner and Hans Asperger: Setting the Historical Record Straight' *JAACAP,* 55[8]:728.

PART 3: THE DARK SIDE OF PSYCHOANALYSIS

In the next section, we will look at the history of psychoanalysis. Despite obvious differences in how various medical specialties apply their practice, none appear to be more controversial than in psychiatry, wherein confident assertions about intangibles have been the purview of psychoanalysis. In this psychiatric specialty, an understanding of an autistic child's inner state is usually attributed to a faulty parent-child relationship. In doing so, psychoanalysis disregards neurodevelopmental aspects of autism and its genetic underpinnings in favor of desires and subconscious yearnings. In a field where the loudest and most histrionic voices gather prominence, fraudsters abound.

The next few chapters detail the rise and fall of a prominent figure within the field of psychoanalysis. Instead of looking at an autistic patient from a psychoanalytic perspective, let's turn the table and take a look at an influential psychoanalyst and the credibility of his treatment philosophy. Overall, the history of psychoanalysis in autism, similar to Rosen's actions, reminds us of an embarrassing and dangerous uncle tarnishing the family's reputation.

The Refrigerator Mothers

The term "refrigerator mothers" was probably first applied to autism by Leo Kanner in the late 1940s when he noted a "genuine lack of maternal warmth", "parental coldness", and children who "were left neatly in refrigerators which did not defrost". Even though Kanner himself abandoned the use of the term, other psychoanalysts adopted the same, using it as a branding iron for useless therapeutic attempts whose scars are still felt today (see France's autism treatment "shame": http://www.bbc.co.uk/news/magazine-17583123).

Two prominent psychoanalysts championed this notion and were primarily responsible for its embrace by the medical profession. Coincidentally, both psychoanalysts greatly exaggerated their credentials and indulged in aggressive physical interventions that even during their time should have been judged as cruel. Most people know about Bruno Bettelheim who compared both autistic children and schizophrenic patients to prisoners in a concentration camp. In this essay we will narrate the biography of the lesser-known but equally controversial John Nathaniel Rosen whose vitriolic writings offered a synoptic view to those of Bruno Bettelheim.

John Nathaniel Rosen (1902–1993) rose to prominence in psychiatry through the 1950s to 1970s with his invention of a therapeutic intervention that he called "direct psychoanalysis." Rosen impressed wealthy patrons, fellow psychiatrists, and the general public with his claims of quick, compassionate cures of schizophrenic patients. His theories, methods, and conduct have recently been detailed. In *Against Therapy* (1993*)* Jeffrey Masson treats Rosen as a prime example for "showing how emotional tyranny is at the heart" of psychotherapy. Edward Dolnick's *Madness on the Couch* (1998) couples Rosen with Harold Searles as fraudulent practitioners of "talk therapy" to treat schizophrenia. Readers interested in full-scale exposes of Rosen's rise and fall might consult these books and Rosen's own *Direct Analysis: Selected Papers* (1953).

John Rosen was born in 1902 and graduated from high school in 1920. After completing the required premed courses at Syracuse University, he earned his M.D. in pathology in 1927 from the George Washington College of Medicine. In a 1981 deposition taken in connection with Rosen's suit against the Miami Herald for alleged slander, he cited a number of positions occupied while he was in general practice in New York: a rotating internship at Cumberland Street Hospital (late 1920s), a two-year internship at Brooklyn Jewish Hospital (1928-1930), six-month clinical training in psychiatry at Brooklyn State Hospital (1939), and a residence at Columbia-Presbyterian Medical Center (1945) when he began practicing psychiatry. Phyllis Friedman, once Rosen's patient and then therapist, reported in 1977 that Rosen claimed he did psychological research and later held the rank of Professor Emeritus at Albert Einstein.

Certification by a New York State licensing agency as a Q.P., Qualified Psychiatrist, was evidently legitimate. However, when contacted by Virginia Snyder, a private investigator later hired by one of Rosen's patients, none of the schools named above found any record of Rosen's service. According to Millen Brand, Rosen did undergo personal psychoanalysis with Dr. Ferdinand Nunberg, president of the New York Psychoanalytic Society. In a rare admission, he states that "my knowledge of psychoanalysis was limited to what I had learned in the first months of my personal analysis and from my reading on the subject," (Rosen 1953, p.3) and in his 1981 deposition, that he had never taken board exams in psychiatry. Throughout his career, Rosen exaggerated his credentials, cure rates, and support while minimizing his responsibility for damaging his clients. Thus, any characterizations of Rosen as a "psychiatrist" or "psychoanalyst" rest on flimsy grounds.

In 1947, Rosen published his most influential paper in *Psychiatric Quarterly*, 'The Treatment of Schizophrenic Psychosis by Direct Analytic Therapy', re-published in *Direct Analysis: Selected Papers* (1953). In this paper, he reports resolving the psychosis of 36 patients suffering from "deteriorated schizophrenia," ranging in age from fifteen to fifty-two. Physicians other than himself, he says, diagnosed his patients' schizophrenia. He purportedly got results in months, even weeks.

A lengthy chart details their symptomatology, types, duration, and (in)effectiveness of prior treatments, and duration of direct psychoanalysis among other details. Viewed closely, the chart reveals egregious flaws in methodology. Interestingly, 24 of his 37 patients were female – almost two thirds, exactly reversing their proportions in the general population: "Approximately two males are affected for every female" (Torrey 2013, p.123). What's more, he does not confirm his "cure" rates with any objective criteria or impartial evaluation. He defines "recovery" subjectively, meaning that, such a degree of integrity is achieved that the emotional stability of the patient and his personality and character structures are so well organized as to withstand at least as much environmental assault as is expected of a normal person, that is, of a person who never experienced a psychotic episode (Rosen 1953, p.46). Examined closely, the apparent "objectivity" of his chart collapses.

Firmly established as a bold and creative innovator, Rosen deeply awed O. Spurgeon English, Chair of the Department of Psychiatry at Temple University Medical School and author of a widely used textbook, Introduction to Psychiatry. Rosen appears to have impressed peers and benefactors alike as charismatic, preternaturally capable, and compassionate. English secured a three-year Rockefeller Brothers grant in 1956 to establish the Institute for Direct Analysis within the Psychiatry Department. With this funding he provided Rosen with three buildings for his practice, treating patients chosen by a committee of two psychiatrists and a psychologist. Three years later, in 1959, English obtained an associate professorship for Rosen. English has disputed Rosen's claim to have been promoted to full professor in 1960, a rank he supposedly held for 12 years until retirement at the age of 70. English told Jeffrey Masson, author of Against Therapy, that Rosen remained an associate professor throughout his career at Temple, leaving in 1965 when English retired.

Rosen's reputation as a creative and effective therapist continued to grow. In 1968, Millen Brand, based an adulatory novel (*Savage Sleep*) on Rosen's work, lavishly praising his approach. A 1970 survey of psychiatrists and psychoanalysts rated Rosen the second of fourteen most controversial living psychiatrists in the United States. In 1971 the American Academy of Psychotherapy named him Man of the Year. Rosen later asserted that the Doris Duke Foundation and Webster Foundation contributed to the support of his Institute, and that the Rockefeller Brothers Foundation and "other benefactors" established his Institute in Doylestown, Pennsylvania – all untrue.

Freud never believed he could cure psychoses with his "talking cure." However, Rosen drew explicitly on Freudian theory, with unique emphases. In "The Perverse Mother" (1953), Rosen blames his patients' mental illness on a lack of maternal love, stunting their normal development in the earliest, oral stage. Twinned with this putative cause is an equation of dreams with psychosis, into which patients have escaped to muffle their anguish at being unloved. The patient's resulting psychosis, he claimed, was an "interminable nightmare." The therapist must awaken the sufferer "by unmasking the real content of his psychosis." In extended exercises of "naive Freudianism," Rosen simplistically labeled his symbolic clients' "productions" with cursory, stock interpretations. Snow-capped mountains were a mother's frozen breasts, he liked to say. He told patients their mother's milk had been sour, that women had incestuous fantasies about or actual encounters with their fathers.

Rosen reported that the mothers of patients often expressed an anguished concern for their sons or daughters, verging on the self-sacrificial. Their protests, he admits, seemingly fly in the face of blame for bad mothering. Yet he has discovered, because he believed his unconscious deeply in tune with that of the patients, the patient recalls the mother's non-verbal cues in the earliest, oral stage of life: the patient remembers an unloving mother's message, saying, in effect, "Be still. Be quiet. Be dead." If schizophrenia stems from disturbances in a patient's earliest infancy, why then does the illness appear in late adolescence or early adulthood? Rosen invokes a Tower of Pisa metaphor. The patient's selfhood was "built on a shallow, uneven foundation." Thus, succeeding stages of development—the onset of puberty, independence, marriage, and parenthood—shake an already faulty structure, leading to collapse. Because bad mothering caused the disease, the therapist must replace her. He must use "cunning, guile, shrewdness, and seductiveness" that are buried in his own unconscious to ferret out the patients' secrets and return them to their pre-psychotic state. To paraphrase, the therapist surrenders to his or her own unconscious, primitive impulses to unravel the patient's conflicts. Rosen suggests his own "capacity for loving" is a "divine gift" enhanced by psychoanalysis. To treat patients left largely "unimproved" by previous treatments, Rosen indicated that the therapist needs a high "degree of inner security." He makes up for his patients' "tremendous deficit of love" by forcefully, lovingly, and informally breaking through their defensive, psychotic shells. Sometimes—quite implausibly—he claimed "bringing the patient up all over again" by spending four to ten hours a day with her for months.

Sprinkled through Rosen's published writings are strong hints of misogyny, an obsessive homophobia, implausible rationales for lies and impostures, and briefs for verbal, physical and sexual abuse of patients. Rosen openly expresses distaste for women who step outside traditional homemaking roles. He attacks their threatening desire to "wear men's clothes, try for commanding positions in business, and prefer not to care for their own children but hire nurses to play the role of make-shift mother" as "a perversion of the maternal instinct." (Rosen 1953, p.101). Time and again he strains at interpretations that purportedly uncover veiled homosexual tendencies. Typically, Rosen uncovers "a homosexual defense against incest temptations and the danger of the lofty position, i.e., manhood." (Rosen 1953, p.31).

To shock patients out of denial, Rosen would tell them he'd once been psychotic himself with the patients' symptoms. He called this device "the trick against the trick." He would assume the roles of priest, mother, or mother-in-law, among others. Or he would stage psychodramas. In one instance, psychiatric aides impersonated as FBI agents to unmask a patient's fantasies of criminal wrongdoing. Another skit led to near-disaster. Confronting a patient believing her father was condemned to death, he brought the family together and announced a spurious reprieve from the governor, followed by a celebration. The patient reacted by refusing to eat and losing 40 pounds. Rosen justified his bizarre roles and enactments as "helping patients re-establish contact with reality."

References

Dolnick E. (1998) *Madness on the Couch*, Simon & Schuster.
Masson J. (1993) *Against Therapy*, Atheneum.
Rosen JN. (1953) *Direct Analysis: Selected Papers*, Grune & Stratton.
Torrey EF (2013) *Surviving Schizophrenia*, Harper Perennial.

Therapy or Patient Abuse?

Despite repeated assurances of his love and solitude for patients, Rosen time and again lost his temper. One patient carried a pillow around with her, rocking it, reading to it, and calling it her son Stevie. Rosen attacked her fantasies: "I grabbed the pillow and banged it on the floor, saying, 'see, that can't be a baby. I threw it on the floor with all my might and it didn't cry'." He argues unconvincingly that his violent, abusive methods appealed "to that tiny portion of the ego that is in contact with reality," inducing the patient "to renounce some of his delusions and hallucinations." Confronting a patient fearful of being cut up and fed to tigers, Rosen blandished a knife and threatened to castrate, kill and eat him. Admitting that "disgusting annoyances" often elicited a "considerable amount of anger and resentment," he and several aides once pinned a long-haired patient to a chair for a haircut. By his "counter-aggressive anger," Rosen hopes to regain the patient's attention for therapeutic ends.

Rosen not only reported physical abuse and coercion in his practice but openly displayed them before audiences. In *Observations on Direct Analysis: The Therapeutic Technique of Dr. John N. Rosen*, Morris W. Brody recounts a dialogue before a group between Rosen and a young woman. Rosen repeatedly demands the woman have intercourse with him, threatening to knock her through a wall. At a meeting attended by a large number of observers, Rosen demeaned and humiliated the young woman as "stupid" and "low class." (Masson 1993, p.152).

The generally favorable comments of six psychoanalysts follow the text of 'The Treatment of Schizophrenic Psychosis' in *Selected Papers*. The eminent internist Paul Federn (who invented the term "direct analysis") finds Rosen's method "in full accordance" with Federn's "assertions in regard to psychoanalysis of psychoses." Yet he doubts that Rosen's "cases are cured in the sense of having been freed of the unknown pathologic entity causing schizophrenic or paranoiac psychosis." (Rosen, 1953, pp.77, 76). Federn also recommends confining experimentation with Rosen's method to "trained psychiatrists who are also fully qualified psychoanalysts". Suggesting Rosen's "cures" might be somewhat ephemeral, Joseph Meiers asks that final judgment on his methods be "reserved for a duration of a few years of maintained cures." Remarkably, Jule Eisenbud finds Rosen "has absolutely no hostility ... toward the psychotic patient," despite blatant evidence to the contrary. Typical among so many of Rosen's colleagues, Hyman Spotnitz gushes uncritically: "It requires a great deal of courage, devotion, and sincerity to do this type of work." (Rosen 1953, p.91). Though most of the panel members called for reassessment of

Rosen's results after five years or so, the profession ignored follow-up studies refuting his claims.

Even after Rosen was officially stripped of his credentials in 1983, his former colleagues failed to fault him. Contacted by Jeffrey Masson in 1986, O. Spurgeon English doggedly defended his previous sponsorship of Rosen and denied the relevance of the charges of abuse to the effectiveness of his methods. Dr. Morris W. Brody admitted growing disillusioned and suspicious of Rosen, recounting an exchange between Rosen and a patient. After repeatedly threatening a patient for insisting she heard voices, Rosen hit her. Brody, however, denied he was being sadistic. Brody questioned Masson's interest in Rosen, blaming his wealthy clients for allowing themselves to be fooled. Rosen's unwavering support from prominent professional colleagues not only during his career but after his disgrace make it difficult to refute Masson's charge that "emotional tyranny is at the heart" of psychotherapy.

Unsurprisingly, Rosen's reputation and influence led many wealthy, prominent families to turn over dysfunctional relatives to him for treatment — usually with no formal legal proceedings. The media baron and ambassador Walter Annenberg placed his son in Rosen's care. While there, the young man shot himself in 1962, an incident which enraged Annenberg. However, the private investigator he hired was unable to penetrate the secrecy surrounding Rosen's operation. Rosen also had custody at various times of Barbara Hooker (related by marriage to the

Rockefellers), Barbara Stuart (wife of the chairman of the Quaker Oats board), and both Anne Morrow Lindberg and her niece Connie Morrow, among others. Treating such patients was extremely lucrative.

In 1983, Rosen voluntarily gave up his medical license to avoid being tried for incompetence and malpractice by the State Board of Medical Education and Licensure of the Department of State of Pennsylvania. His disgrace raises intriguing questions. Was Rosen, as Millen Brand suggests, initially a sincere but misguided self-promoter? If so, did easy wealth seduce him into neglecting and abusing his patients, placing them in the hands of brutal, untrained assistants? Or was he criminally negligent, even sadistic and corrupt, from the outset of his career? The record clearly supports the latter. A series of lawsuits attacked Rosen beginning in the 1960s for fraud and violence, several patients died in his custody, and careful studies exposed the inefficacy of his treatment. Yet neither government agencies or officials, medical societies, nor parents of patients intervened effectively to restrain or punish him. Rosen asserted his "assistant therapists would generally be people with degrees in psychology up to even a doctor, doctorate" (1983, deposition, p.16). However, his so-called "assistant therapists", as a rule, were often former patients, untrained and uncredentialed despite Rosen's protests. Brand commented that after Rosen "had cured those [patients], he used them for nurses and attendants", a practice Rosen announced in 1947. More bluntly, Dr. Isidor Scherer of the Department of Public Welfare repeated Rosen's comment, "I will not hire anybody unless he's an ex-nut."

Hiring patients or individuals for supportive health services who are not licensed or certified by a health profession regulatory board is now illegal in many states (Niesz, 2001)

References

Brody MW. (1959) *Observations on Direct Analysis: The Therapeutic Technique of Dr. John N. Rosen, NY: Vantage Press.*

Masson J. (1993) *Against Therapy*, Atheneum.

Niesz, (2001) States' Criminal Background Check for long-term care (https://www.cga.ct.gov/2001/rpt/2001-R-0753.htm)_

Roosen JN. (1953) *Direct Analysis: Selected Papers*, Grune & Stratton.

Fraud

The trail of debunking studies and lawsuits begins early. In 1958, William Horwitz and three other psychiatrists identified 19 patients of the 37 Rosen claimed to have cured. They found that seven of them had never been diagnosed as schizophrenic. Of the twelve schizophrenics, all had relapsed and been readmitted to mental hospitals, some repeatedly. None had been cured. After their three-year grant to Temple expired in 1959, the Rockefeller Brothers Foundation evaluated the effectiveness of Rosen's approach and found no significant difference between his treatment and a control group. A group of four psychiatrists reached a similar conclusion in 1966, reporting: "This evaluative study indicates that a group of patients treated by the method of 'direct analysis' did not show significantly better results than a random control group or a designated control group" (Bookhammer et al. 1966). Yet these repeated danger signals failed to dent Rosen's growing reputation among his peers and clients.

Along with unmistakable signs pointing to Rosen's flawed methodology came brushes with the law. In 1960, two years before the death of Walter Annenberg's son, Rosen lost a case known as Hammer v. Rosen in New York. In his defense, Rosen argued "that the treatment was knowingly and freely consented to by reason of the fact that the patient's mother testified that if beating was a means of cure, she was agreeable to the treatment." Mrs. Hammer disagreed, testifying that her daughter returned from treatments "black and blue." Without producing any expert witnesses, Rosen said the "beating" was a recognized form of treatment. He was indicted in 1972 for income tax evasion for the years of 1965, 1966 and 1967. In response he pled "no contest" and paid a fine of $10,000. In 1979, a patient of his named Claudia Ehrmann was beaten to death by two of Rosen's untrained aides who were supposedly treating her with "conflict therapy." When criminal charges were filed, Rosen's attorneys agreed to settle out of court for $100,000. Rosen was unrepentant: "It's not costing me a thing." (Rosen, deposition, p.16)

As early as 1959, when support ended for his Institute at Temple, Rosen built several houses at a facility called Twin Silos near Doylestown, Bucks County, Pennsylvania. He called these houses psychiatric intensive units, placing one or two patients in each one along with attendants who lived with them. The reality was more sinister: many of these houses included "security rooms" where patients were confined without heat or toilet facilities, stripped, restrained or beaten. Later investigations and court documents reveal that Rosen spent the winter months each year in Boca Raton, leaving some patients at Twin Silos with untrained aides and taking others with him, though he was not licensed to practice in Florida. He successfully gained certification to "advise and counsel" clients in Boca Raton, then lost it when authorities discovered he had listed a non-existent address for the facility and could not explain exactly what services he intended to render. Though he continued to charge exorbitant fees for patients placed in his custody, Rosen neglected them, reportedly spending the bulk of his time on the golf course or visiting his stockbroker.

The beginning of the end for Rosen dates from 1977, when a former patient, Sally Zinman, voiced serious concerns. Sally was born in Philadelphia in 1937, the adopted daughter of a prominent local banker. As a well-educated adjunct English instructor at Queens College, New York, since 1964, she awoke one day in October 1970, having apparently experienced transient global amnesia: a sudden episode of severe memory loss and confusion that generally happens for no apparent reason. Several months later, after a cursory examination by psychiatrist Harvey Gorman, her father chartered a plane, flew her to Boca Raton, and placed her in the care of Rosen, a golfing partner. After a rather pleasant month, Sally asked Rosen to move into her parents' apartment and see him daily. After apparently agreeing, Rosen and an aide tore off most of her clothes, beat her, and tied her to a bed in a security room for twenty-four hours. Despite futile efforts to escape, Sally remained in Rosen's custody for two more years with her parents' collusion, enduring sexual molestation for which she was too frightened to resist. She gained her freedom in 1973.

Several years later, Sally hired Virginia Snyder, an award-winning investigative reporter with a well-earned reputation for integrity and gritty tenacity. In the course of her investigations, Virginia learned that an elderly patient, Ted Schwartz, had died on June 13, 1977, in the same room Sally had been held in. Rosen belatedly signed the death certificate. Snyder sent documented information about Rosen's abuses to all the regulatory and policing agencies in Florida and Pennsylvania. The energy and scope of Snyder's efforts were initially futile. The failure of Rosen's colleagues and their professional societies to restrain or discipline him were matched by the remarkable timidity of all the authorities she contacted: none found reason to act.

In September 1977, Tim Pallesen, a staff writer for the Miami Herald, Palm Beach Edition, reported on Rosen's physical abuse of Sally Zinman and another patient, Julia Blythe. The article was confirmed later in the year by The Philadelphia Inquirer, which raised question about Ted Schwartz's death based on an affidavit filed by Merry Humose, a former patient and aide of Rosen's. Rosen filed suit against Pallesen, the Miami Herald and the Philadelphia Inquirer, resulting in a remarkably revealing deposition by Rosen giving his version of events. (Bookhammer 1966) Despite a tissue of lies and evasions which interlaces the document, Rosen alludes to sexual involvements with his patients — activity which is not only illegal but suggests that Rosen had long since crossed the line separating normality and patient abuse. The suit was settled out of court for Rosen's attorney's fees.

Two years later, in December 1979, a thirty-one-year-old patient, Claudia Ehrman, was found dead in her room at Rosen's Boca Raton facility. In Rosen's absence, one aide, Robin Samuels, held Ehrman's feet while another, Jay Patete, kneed her in the abdomen so brutally that he lacerated her liver, killing her. Both aides received light sentences — probation — and the Rosen's insurance company paid. When the police tried to remove two remaining patients from Rosen's facility, the parents successfully resisted, partly justifying Dr. Brody's charge of parental folly. Far too often, parents colluded with Rosen in keeping their relatives in his custody or returning them when they managed to break free.

A year and a half later, another patient Janet Katkow sued Rosen in Bucks County Pennsylvania. While in his custody from 1970 until 1979, Rosen continually abused her sexually, undressing and forcing her to suck his penis literally hundreds of times while he vapidly philosophized: "This is what it is all about, this is when a baby is at peace, when it is sucking." When she invariably vomited, he rationalized her revulsion as vomiting up her mother's bad milk. His "therapy" moved to include forcing her to lick his anus and consume his faeces, engaging in three-way sex and cunnilingus with another woman under threat of violence, and enforced sex with an elderly judge in a putative attempt to cure the judge's impotence.

In 1983, the State Board of Medical Education and Licensure of the Department of State of Pennsylvania accused Rosen of sixty-seven violations of the Pennsylvania Medical Practices Act, and thirty-five violations of rules and regulations of the Medical Board. The citation mentions abuses of Sally Zinman, Janet Katkow, as well as another patient Julia Bythe, who was imprisoned by Rosen for sixteen years, from 1963 to 1979, during which she was continually abused sexually. According to the citation, several other women complained of sexual abuse, and the Board cited enforced homosexual acts involving minors. Rosen was also charged with keeping Michael Hallinan bound and shackled in a security room, whose existence was confirmed by several other patients. Despite the damning nature of the evidence as indicated by the citation, the Board heard a complaint that the consent agreement left out evidence that Rosen sexually and physically abused patients. Moreover, their unwillingness to fine or imprison him - congratulating themselves on avoiding a costly hearing—fit the pattern of official reluctance to restrain or punish Rosen.

References

Bookhammer RS. et al. (1966) 'A five-year clinical follow-up study of schizophrenics treated by Rosen's 'Direct Analysis' compared with controls.' *American Journal of Psychiatry*, 123: 602-604

The Direct Psychoanalytical Institute

Over the years, I have had the good fortune of interviewing several people who witnessed Rosen's practice, either as patients or as managers within his health centers. This section details my interview with Will in regard to events that transpired during the downfall of Dr. Rosen from 1968-1970. Will is an assumed name as he preferred to remain anonymous for the purpose of this book. However, Will reviewed the accompanying narrative and made the necessary corrections to make it as accurate as possible according to his recollection.

In 1967, Will was a freshman at a Pennsylvania college majoring in Psychology, when one morning he read an ad in the newspaper requesting an assistant to a psychiatrist. The ad made him curious enough to embark on a one-hour ride away from Philadelphia for a job interview. Will arrived for his interview in Gardenville, PA where two houses served as treatment centers for the Direct Psychoanalytic Institute (DPI) of Dr. John Rosen. Both houses appeared austere: one had red shingles and the other green, with little or no landscaping or vegetation. There, Will met Dr. Charles Sullivan, a protégé and confidant of Dr. Rosen's. The interview went well and 2 days afterwards Will received a telephone call offering him the position. Will would work there 24/7 and receive $75 per week, an amount which seemed more than enough considering he had no other expenses. The units also received a $100 food allowance per week. The job started that very same day! Will still remembers vividly that first night, hearing the screams of a female patient threatening to cut his penis off. Will was so alarmed that he moved the dresser to block the door as he went to sleep.

Dr. Rosen was at the treatment centers primarily for meetings with the patient's parents as they dropped off their loved one. The patients were invariably the rich and famous. Will was sometimes blown away by those who would come through the door. Besides the visiting Dr. Rosen and Dr. Sullivan, there were usually two assistants, like himself, for each treatment center. Dr. Sullivan, for the most part, acted on behalf of Dr. Rosen. Although Sullivan represented himself as a doctor; it was later discovered that Sullivan was working on his dissertation but had never completed his doctorate work. According to Will, Sullivan was a learned man and skilled psychotherapist, who could easily pass himself off as a doctor.

After that first year, Will decided to take 2 years off from college in order to continue, what he thought would be a great educational opportunity. During Will's time at the DPI, there were 6 or so treatment units in Gardenville and other, close by, locations. In reality, Will understood that he was acting as a caretaker, friend and companion to the patients and occasionally provided entertainment by taking them to a movie. Will stated that his services and support were primarily needed during the first couple of weeks after the patients were brought in, when, according to instructions from Dr. Rosen, the undergraduate assistants were supposed to immediately dispose of all of the patient's prescribed medications. This lack of a sensible titration (cold turkey withdrawal) prompted psychotic behaviors in the patients, lasting from days to several weeks in some cases. Patients underwent a radical, intense and often violent state, during their withdrawal from a combination of drugs which commonly included Valium, Lithium, Thorazine, Stelazine, etc. The sudden withdrawal from Valium, it was later discovered, risked having life threatening seizures, although no seizures were ever witnessed by him. According to Will, suddenly cutting off their medications in that way produced a temporary "raw insanity" from the patients that inadvertently proved to be a small window to their mental problems. However, in other cases their sudden drug withdrawal prompted hallucinations and screaming for which many of them had to be restrained.

Not surprisingly, some patients would manage to run away, disappearing until days later when their parents would call Dr. Rosen saying that they had somehow returned home; often traveling long distances from the treatment center. Dr. Sullivan would have Will along with other assistants, take a hired plane and fly to the nearest airport to the patient from where they would take a limo to the patient's home residence. There, always in the middle of the night, they would overpower the sleeping patient, place him in a straitjacket and bring him back to the institute. They did this 3 times for different patients. Will said this was a very scary experience, for the patient and for them. He questioned to himself, the legality of forcibly picking up patients and crossing state lines.

Will described Dr. Rosen as a man in his 60's who was somewhat overweight and short of stature. He was an aggressive and accusative individual who rarely had anything nurturing to say. He came off as a tyrant. If he thought he could read you, he would immediately attack your weaknesses in the most aggressive way possible. When first meeting Will, who was thin and had shoulder length hair at the time, Rosen remarked that "they should have listened to me in New York when I told them that all men wanted to be women." Will said that the remark was meant to disarm him but had the effect of convincing him that Rosen had apparent hang-ups about his own physical attributes. Seemingly in-keeping with his acerbic personality, Rosen enjoyed the use of verbal "shock therapy" although the technique would tend to alienate his assistants and, usually, the patients as well.

While half of the "assistant psychotherapists" at the Gardenville centers were women, many were former patients, some still receiving treatment, and who were retained in service by Dr. Rosen. Will had spoken to several of them during conversations as they transitioned from patients to gainful employees. Invariably the former female patients told similar stories about their therapy. They said that there were instances when during their "treatment" Rosen would direct them to remove all of their clothes and lay on the floor of his office in order "to strip away their inhibitions and receive his therapy." Will kept these stories under his vest for almost 50 years. Given Dr. Rosen's limited physical attributes and character flaws, Will wondered whether the nude therapy was an attempt to overcome the doctor's own sexual fixations, or whether Rosen was just a "dirty old man"?

During treatment, Rosen and Sullivan would speak in the most rudimentary Freudian terms, especially when addressing the patients who often seemed oblivious of them. Rosen and Sullivan were also fond of play-acting which Rosen called "acting in", where they might address Freudianesque fixations like the "castration complex" by bringing patients to the office and having them pull down their drawers. Rosen would then pull a real looking sword and place the patients through a castration scenario. Will seldom witnessed positive results after this embarrassing and intimidating fiasco. Effective psychoanalysis needed positive transference between physician and patient, and unfortunately the only transference of any kind was between the patient and Will, as, at the end of the day, he was the only one there. Dr. Rosen, in turn, seemed to create barriers rather than positive transference. He seemed to bully his way into the thinking processes of patients, while proffering confusing insults and frightening tactics.

The last "treatment center" that remained, south of Gardenville, after 1970, was overseen by Will. The relatives of the patients were paying thousands of dollars per week while the Direct Psychoanalytic Institute's care deteriorated, ultimately becoming nonexistent. Will had witnessed patients quickly returned to their guardians when payments would be withheld. Will had a growing empathy for the problems of Dr. Rosen's patients, many of them seemingly medication related. He claimed that many of the patients, once not extremely medicated, would return to a fragile state of normalcy. Their problems fixated on common issues in their growing up and their parenting, or lack thereof.

Dr. Rosen disappeared from sight around late 1969. Will, with the aid of another assistant psychotherapist, oversaw the last few patients. In the end, Rosen's Direct Psychoanalytic Institute was a collapsed organization. Will had to drive the last three patients to their homes in Florida, Philadelphia and New York and explain to the parents that there was no longer any treatment.

Will continued his education, eventually specializing in addiction therapy, and ultimately that was the field he entered as a profession. He hoped that at some point that he would get credit for the work he had already done for Rosen, but records of the Direct Psychoanalytic Institute could not be found.

Will recently retired, ended his career as an addiction counselor. In concluding the interview Will said, "At the end Dr. Rosen seemed to be a miserable man. An unhappy man who enjoyed making people squirm. His best outcomes, in those last days, were all but achieved unknowingly."

PART 4: MISCELLANEOUS

In this last section I would like to introduce myself to the reader. In writing about Salt Lake City (SLC), I am writing about my family. When my grandson was diagnosed with syndromic autism, I recommended moving my family to Salt Lake City. The Autism unit at the University was directed by a good friend of mine and I knew about the public services and special education resources in the city. I could not have been more impressed. Unfortunately, Dr. Ed Ritvo who initiated many of the epidemiological studies conducted at SLC recently died. Ed was a towering figure in the autism community. By including this section in the book, I just wanted to let Ed know that he still lives in my mind.

The last section is one about St. Elizabeths Hospital, my training ground within the National Institute of Mental Health. I greatly appreciate the efforts of all my mentors who molded my academic career. They walked the walk; teaching by example. I am still amazed that I was able to breath the history of psychiatry in a hospital that befitted pious behavior towards our patients.

Salt Lake City and its Role in the History of Autism

Salt Lake City was founded in 1847 by Mormon pioneers led by Bringham Young. This led to a homogenous society based on irrigation agriculture that kept genealogical records on its citizens from the city's inception until present. The Family History Library in downtown Salt Lake City is advertised as the genealogical capital of the world. The tightly knit societal structure and copious records lend themselves to studies of genetic and environmental factors as they modify occurrence rates of specific medical conditions.

Although unknown to many individuals, Salt Lake City (SLC), Utah has played a major role in the history of autism within our country. As a result of a responsive state government and a generous community SLC boasts the presence of a Spectrum Academy that covers elementary, middle and high school years with a population of over 500 students. Carmen B Pingree, a major figure in the field of autism, established her headquarters to fight for the rights of autistic individuals in the living room of her home in Salt Lake City. In her honor, a center for learning dedicated to supporting families of autistic individuals now bears her name. For those in need of special services, the local government provides for in-home visits that include physical/occupational therapy and speech pathology. Furthermore, the Kosair Pediatric Hospital at SLC is one of the best in the nation. Not the least of advantages, the University of Utah boasts an integrated clinic specializing in autism spectrum disorder. I have been fortunate enough to have attended the inaugural festivities for the Autism Spectrum Academy, visited the Kosair Clinics and have established close working relationships with the members of the Autism Clinic at the University of Utah. When my daughter was looking for a city that would be supportive of the needs of my grandson, I never hesitated in recommending SLC.

At present, however, I would like to talk about the role SLC played in autism research and in clarifying many misconceptions about autism. The story begins in the 1980s and it still unfolding. It centers around Ed Ritvo, a major figure in the field of autism, who made his academic career while at the University of California, Los Angeles (UCLA). Back then the UCLA Department of Psychiatry was known as the Department of the Ed's, both for Ed Ritvo and Ed Ornitz. It is fortunate that the interests of these two individuals focused on pervasive developmental disorders with Dr. Ornitz being inclined to pursue the nature of syndromic (often genetic) cases and Ritvo trying to answer epidemiological questions.

Although UCLA had great resources for pursuing most types of research, this was not the case for epidemiological studies. In the 1980s Los Angeles had a population boom that made it difficult to perform epidemiological studies that had to canvas or sample a large percentage of the population. The large number of hospitals and social services agencies provided a logistical nightmare when trying to coordinate any type of research effort among them. It was then that Ed Ritvo met Carmen Pingree who had gone to UCLA in order to get her son evaluated. Carmen was from Salt Lake City where most of the population lived on a narrow geographical corridor that made it rather easy to contact them. Furthermore, a significant percentage of their inhabitants belonged to the Church of Jesus Christ of the Later Days (Mormons) and as part of their religious affiliation the genealogical tree of the population had been carefully preserved across many generations.

Dr. Ritvo used Carmen's local connections to establish headquarters in SLC for the most comprehensive epidemiological study to date. After screening the majority of the population and identifying potential cases, members of Ritvo's team examined them. The results of the examination along with answers to a screening survey of Dr. Ornitz (consisting of 500 questions) allowed for the identification of 241 cases of autism. Seventeen of these families had two children affected, one family had three, one had four, and one had five autistic children. It was noteworthy that when the parents were interviewed, they seemed to fall within the spectrum, some with subtle symptoms, others with a definite diagnosis. Despite the large number of individuals in these families, the odds ratio for a sibling having autism was calculated as being only 10%. It may be important to note that this odds ratio may have been artifactually lowered as many families with an autistic child seemingly decided to stop procreation immediately after their child received a diagnosis. (Ritvo, 2005)

It is striking that such an important study received acerbic criticisms from journal reviewers. According to Dr. Ritvo, the publication was rejected seven times before finally being accepted. Back then a common misconception was that autistic children would not be able to grow up, get married and have children. Besides battling these misconceptions the study underlined other important findings. In very detailed analysis, autistic children as compared to neurotypicals had the same rate of colds, ear infections, allergies, vaccinations, immune deficiencies, celiac and digestive disorders. Although a lot has been said about vaccines and immune deficiencies in autism, the UCLA-Utah study found no evidence that these were correlated.

Another major finding of the early study was the heterogeneity of symptoms in affected individuals. Although some exhibited symptoms of classical Kanner's autism others were quite subtle. These subtle cases were called subclinical or "forme frustres".

The original study is still ongoing and occasional publications of this cohort have appeared over the years. These ongoing studies have revealed that often "classical" cases can transform into the subtle variants (Asperger). In this regard Dr. Ritvo was a strong advocate that Asperger and autism differ in severity but not in kind. More recently the study of Dr. Ritvo has prompted other researchers to study the genetics of families having more than one affected individual. In this regard Dr. Ritvo's legacy will keep growing over the years.

References:

Ritvo ER. (2005) *Understanding the Nature of Autism and Asperger's Disorder*. Jessica Kingsley Publishers.

Memories of St. Elizabeths Hospital

When autism was first described, those patients that received the diagnosis were invariably surrendered to the care of the state at large psychiatric hospitals. Kanner disapproved of this practice, in part, based on his experience with Donald Tripplett (incept case of his clinical series). Early on, Donald was institutionalized and painfully regressed in his condition only to flourish when his family took him back home. Curiously, many patients that are institutionalized, regardless of diagnosis, usually develop autistic-like behaviors. It almost seems that these autistic behaviors are of use (adaptive) in the institutional setting but maladaptive in the social environment. My own experiences while working in such an institution were quite positive. I have fond memories of my service and feel both humbled and honored to have partaken a portion of my career in this setting. In the following paragraphs I share some of my memories with the reader.

Some 35 years ago, as a young officer for the Public Health Service, I was stationed at St. Elizabeths Hospital. This was one of the first generations of American mental asylums created by the lobbying efforts of Dorothea Dix in the mid-1800s. In its heydays, St. Elizabeths Hospital was a walled city upon itself. Boasting of having a small railroad, a fire station, and furniture workshop it fulfilled all needs to its thousands of psychiatric patients. A scenic point in the grounds had the highest elevation in Washington, DC. Years before my work there, St. Elizabeths was surrounded by a plush polish neighborhood.

National policies in the late 1800s and early 1900s were meant to keep patients secluded and outside the normal discourse of society. This would change in the 1950s with the introduction of powerful anti-psychotic agents like Thorazine (chlorpromazine). Why spend all that money with institutionalization when drugs could do the work for society? Wishful thinking propitiated a wave of patients being released from mental institutions into the community. These patients often had little or no social contacts, no money, and only a bag of drugs to carry with them. Patients never integrated into their communities, remaining homeless but keeping themselves close to the hospital to which they were dependent for medication. The once plush neighborhood of St. Elizabeths thus transformed to a crime ridden slum.

In the 1980s, we still had many patients at St. Elizabeths Hospital, including a cohort that had been lobotomized by Walter Freeman. A neurologist by training, Feeman had been mesmerized by the behavioral results observed after cutting white matter nerve fibers within the prefrontal lobe (*leukotomy*) by Nobel prize winner Antonio Egas Moniz. To perfect his procedure, Freeman associated himself with a neurosurgeon by the name of James Watts. Both Watts and Freeman were faculty members at the George Washington University School of Medicine. Together they developed a rather aggressive procedure to sever even more of the white matter in the prefrontal lobes. The procedure was renamed lobotomy and the surgical technique that they standardized was known as the *Freeman-Watts procedure*. Thousands of patients ended receiving lobotomies, including Rosemary Kennedy (sister of late President John F. Kennedy).

Freeman modified the lobotomy procedure on his own using an ice pick and local anesthesia to approach the prefrontal lobe through the thin bone of the eye socket. Watt adamantly opposed the procedure and thought that Freeman was unqualified to oversee the surgery by himself. Their disagreement led to Watts leaving the practice they had jointly established. In 1969, Watts retired from The George Washington University Hospital. Although retired, I met him several times while visiting some of his ex-patients at St. Elizabeths Hospital. Watts wanted to see if he could still be of help to his patients. I guess this was his way of atoning for past mistakes.

After Watts' death, many of the lobotomized patients made their way to the Blackburn Laboratory. This was the first medical facility at the hospital dedicated to the study of mental illness. Dr. Isaac Wright Blackburn was appointed to St. Elizabeths in 1884 and, because of the patient population, became specialized in the gross pathology of the brain.

Throughout the years the laboratory initially established by Blackburn had many directors, none more famous (or should I say infamous) than Walter Freeman. The young neurologist had left his hometown of Philadelphia and relocated to Washington, DC in 1924. Taking over the Blackburn Laboratory the autopsy suite soon became a theater for entertainment. He performed thousands of autopsies primarily of schizophrenic patients. Decades after leaving his position at St. Elizabeths Hospital, Freeman would donate copies of his written works to the hospital, with the inscription, "To St. Elizabeths Hospital, where I worked 1924-1933, to find some answers to the problem of mental disorder, and where more problems arose than were ever answered".

Of some 15,000 autopsies performed at St. Elizabeths Hospital about 1,500 brains were preserved in a brain/tissue collection. The specimens are of major importance as many of them predate the use of psychopharmacological drugs that often pose a confound to pathological studies. It can also serve to document the effects of treatment by electroshock, metrazol (high doses causing convulsions), insulin shock, and lobotomy. Unfortunately, sometime in the 1990s the brain collection was transferred, along with other similar resources, to a storage facility. Without any upkeep, many of the microscopic slides may have dried and become useless.

Freeman worked hand-in-hand with another neuropathologist, Meta Neumann. Although she retired in 1981, she continued to join us in different congresses, usually choosing to seat in the back row in the company of her husband Robert Cohn. They were always holding hands and Robert was very protective of her. She remained quite lucid during aging and died after her hundredth birthday.

Most of the buildings were closed by the time I joined the staff at St. Elizabeths. I worked at the William A. White building, a research bastion for the NIMH being named for one of St. Elizabeths Hospital superintendents. I started to work under Richard J Wyatt a psychiatrist who made important contributions to the biochemistry of schizophrenia. Dr. Wyatt had been an early survivor of Hodgkin's disease but then went on to develop Burkitt's lymphoma and finally died in a battle with lung cancer. In his obituary, it is said, "His [Wyatt's] program at NIMH probably resulted in the spawning of more scientists devoted to understanding the biology of schizophrenia than any other program in the history of medical research". Dr. Wyatt was dyslexic and faced serious difficulties in writing. He never outgrew his dyslexia but certainly overcame the same. I greatly admired him.

Richard Wyatt was married to Kay Redfield Jamison a clinical psychologist who held the position of professor at the Department of Psychiatry at the John Hopkins Hospital. Kay was one of the best doctors in the United States and chosen by Time magazine as a *Hero of Medicine*. She received a diagnosis of bipolar disorder during adolescence and, later on, co-wrote the classic textbook *Manic Depressive Illness*. Having trained initially at John Hopkins before moving to the NIMH I had the great pleasure of having met both sides of the family.

It is a small world. I would not like to end this narrative without mentioning one of our most distinguished visitors, Dr. Janice Stevens. Early in life she had been a hippie crisscrossing the country by hitchhiking. She claimed a lucky star as nothing bad happened to her. Years later, and if memory serves me correct, she became the first female graduate from the Department of Psychiatry at Harvard Medical School. She then followed her education with a fellowship in Switzerland doing electroencephalography (EEG) and then traveled to India where a particular researcher was doing invasive EEG recordings in schizophrenic patients. Janice loved India and took it upon herself to institute a program on contraceptives throughout rural parts of the country. Her initiatives were not well received by the government and Janise was promptly expelled. She then moved to Africa where she established over 20 schools for underprivileged children. Whenever she came back to the U.S., she would collect money for her children.

Janice was a distinguished scientist with some 100 publications written primarily as a first author. She was a good friend of Paul Maclean, of Triumvirate brain fame, and we used to meet in social gatherings regularly. Our discussions would gyrate about the role of evolution in designing of the brain. We all thought that evolution had been a tinkerer and that any paradigmatic shift had been caused by adding to a preexisting structure rather than a *de novo* design. Overall, the brain is not as efficient as many people think.

There were numerous stories about Janice Stevens, including some that made her out to be a CIA agent. According to Joseph Wortis, the perennial editor for the Biological Psychiatry Journal, it seems that whenever the United States was involved in an international conflict, Janice had been there. This extended all the way till modern times and the invasion of Grenada. Joseph was an old fashion editor who would take telephone calls and do a lot of editing himself with little in terms of delegating authority.

I was honored that Janice came to visit my home in Georgia for a few weeks. She served as an example to my daughters, all of whom adored her. Later on in life, I used to attend congresses with Janice and served as her companion. She was having mental problems and needed somebody to reassure her. During the years I have had the curious distinction of having to sit with prominent neuroscientists in order to prevent them from falling asleep and snoring (think Nobel Prize winner) or getting them through challenging environment like train stations. No matter our achievements, aging provides a common denominator to us all.

References

Linda Wheeler (April 11, 1995) 'A most unusual brain trust.' *The Washington Post*. This article was based in part on an interview I participated along with my friend Archie Fobbs who served as the curator of the Yakovlev-Haleem brain collection.

CONCLUSION

What have we learned since Kanner planted the seed of autism in public consciousness? Has our understanding evolved with time? I would have to answer both questions in a positive manner. We presently know that the prevalence of autism is much more common than first imagined by Kanner. However, many of Kanner's original observations have held true. Autism is now recognized as a lifelong condition that derives from the abnormal development of the nervous system. It is a condition defined by behaviors that manifest themselves during infancy or early childhood. Symptoms vary from patient to patient, either in type, severity or onset. In this regard, any imposed ascertainment value for symptoms bears little consistency among patients and make predictions or generalizations difficult to sustain. Indeed, comparisons among series having small patient numbers, like those reported by Kanner and Asperger, are difficult to interpret. In essence, both Kanner and Asperger emphasized different aspects of symptomatology in a condition characterized by a spectrum of symptoms. Symptom variability is at the source of many controversies in autism. This variability has made it difficult to generalize findings and to interpret the relationship between autism and other neurodevelopmental conditions. The engendered controversies have been disruptive elements which, from a positive perspective, have allowed us to grow and modify our opinions. The critical and self-reflective examinations by patient advocates, such as Leo Kanner and Bernard Rimland, have proven crucial in advancing public awareness of autism.

Kanner's autism is also known as early infantile autism because his definition remained closely tied to a neurodevelopmental condition. Modern genetic studies on the concordance of monozygotic twins support Kanner's views. Alternatively, Asperger's assertion of autism as a personality disorder, albeit lauded by neurodiversity proponents, has not been supported by evidence-based science. Furthermore, his clinical series may have been biased by the culling of patients under precepts enacted by the Nazi regime.

Autism is a syndrome characterized by several core diagnostic features. Normally, when a syndrome is linked to a known cause, it becomes accepted as a disease. Most cases of autism, about 85%, are "idiopathic" in that they lack a known cause, and we are unaware of the specific mechanisms that brings it to existence. In this regard autism is a diagnosis of exclusion. Those cases with a known cause (genetic or environmental exposure) are labelled as secondary. The latter usually exhibit more behavioral problems and comorbidities (e.g., intellectual disability) than the idiopathic cases. Common comorbidities in autism include sleep, mood, and gastrointestinal disorders.

Given the relatively late clinical description of autism, variability of symptoms, and abundance of comorbidities, it is easy to see why the history of autism is one of diagnostic confusion. This is more so the case when you consider that autism, as well as other mental disorders such as schizophrenia, are usually diagnosed by ruling out other mental health disorders. There are no laboratory diagnostic tests or biological markers for either autism or schizophrenia. A diagnosis for these conditions relies on the characteristic clinical picture. In schizophrenia, as in autism, the clinical presentation may include problems with thinking, behaviors, and emotions.

When schizophrenia manifests in childhood (usually defined as before 13 years of age) it provides for a lifelong disorder with a poor outcome. Initially, these children go through a prodromal phase characterized by an autistic withdrawal from daily life activities and odd movements. Adding to the diagnostic confusion, the risk for an autistic individual developing comorbid schizophrenia is 3-4 times that of the general population.

If controversies entail subjects of ongoing discussion, the reader has learned that there are many controversies in autism. Many of them are easy to understand when autism is considered a spectrum of conditions with varying causes and clinical presentations. Others appear more difficult to reconcile when they acquire a significant media dimension that becomes amplified by social/digital technology and emotional appeals. Controversies, in this regard, can grow uncontrollably. The ensuing state of affairs is not one of ignorance or asymmetry of information but, rather, one where a very wide diversity of opinions exists - even between stakeholders. Under such circumstances it is wise not to draw a line to cross the Rubicon. Controversies in autism reflect our multicultural heritage, one that when taken appropriately, allows the opportunity to ask the right questions, apply corrective measures, and grow from the experience.

About Author

Manuel F. Casanova M.D is a medical professional trained in Neurology, Neuropathology and Psychiatry. He specialized in treating children with developmental conditions. Dr. Casanova introduced the use of transcranial magnetic stimulation (TMS) to autism and served as an endowed chair in psychiatry for different academic institutions. He has served as a patient advocate and has carried legislative, digital and communal efforts to improve the life of his patients. His efforts have been rewarded by numerous appointments (e.g., honorary professorships) academic awards and distinctions by parent-based support organizations.

COMING SOON

TALKING ABOUT AUTISM: (2)
Understanding Symptoms and Behaviors.

Autism is a behaviorally diagnosed disorder wherein affected individuals share some core symptoms but manifest them in different forms and degrees. When symptoms are unrecognized and unmanaged, they may lead to externalizing behaviors and autistic burnout. In this regard, early diagnosis can improve the quality of life of those affected.

This book will provide short vignettes that dissect the different symptoms of autism. This exposition will help to recognize the symptoms, propitiate a better understanding as to their nature, and allow for early intervention.

www.ingramcontent.com/pod-product-compliance
Lightning Source LLC
Chambersburg PA
CBHW071716020426
42333CB00017B/2287